2023 ANTHOLOGY

Broken Sleep Books is a working-class indie publisher putting access to the arts at the forefront of what we do. We continue to endeavour to dismantle gentrification within creative arts industries, and one of the core principles of Broken Sleep is in our desire to ensure we are involved in community action: Whether fundraising, mentoring, our giving away books to those in need.

Selected Anthologies from Broken Sleep Books

2023 Anthology

Edited by:
Aaron Kent & Stuart McPherson

ISBN: 978-1-916938-97-7

Cover designed by Aaron Kent

Edited by Aaron Kent & Stuart McPherson

Typeset by Aaron Kent

Broken Sleep Books Ltd
Rhydwen
Talgarreg
Ceredigion
SA44 4HB

Broken Sleep Books Ltd
Fair View
St Georges Road
Cornwall
PL26 7YH

Contents

POETRY

January

Bitter Incoherence

Situation astonishment: stuplifying mutually semantic readership:
bored text benefitting specific poetics: connotes Terrapolis
urgency: joy urgency: word urgency: necessitates conceived collective:

meaningful sublime [crucially thought-time] repurposing
profound possessive metaphoric action: temporarily active
fabulation: individualism standing: poet considerations save
paralysed response: think some-*thing* complex.

Linguistic-litter-pickers: trash-weavers: Earth seeming "what":
spatially complex thing:

coherence symbiosis: temporal losses being human-exceptionalist
idea: approach thick useful wor[l]ds
[well all-things]
proximity to progress opposite language concepts
[play *gains* things]
worlding-with infusing fast-paced inability with slow poets
[rhythm relies language]

branch thinking needs reader filaments: reader-thought [all-
ways]: tradition needs poetics itself: poetic sense being departure:
to be hyphenated poet oddkin: to be corruptive history:
to not get it
trouble times exhaust powers
[play coherence]
capitalist audience
[unsustainable]

difficult is- language: composted audience-of-the-failing: earth-
draining fabulation: text isn't- problem practice: What.

Narrative models access: drawing stand-in view lines:
accessibility alike completion: here being completed becomes:
non-vertiginous.

Sympoietic grammar systems producing trouble space: slow
boundaries reaching an outward tentacular dynamic: boredom
disciplines: digging terms: one text: technical.

A parsing paradox becoming-with Hyphae: reader looped poets:
braided holobionts: enacting self-defined navigation: creating
collectively beneficial models.

Language reaching down entering critters: a trace in thought-time
of human involution: channelling codex through the public.
Involuting thickness

Blight

Panoptic fractal observing
leaked sources - of light
streaming - split reflecting
glitters: "This down here
is where it is". The phrases
are outrunning the grammar.

To be thrust upward at
an angle denoting the
original shape - at access -
is to engage with the
potentiality of a mismatched
interlock; as the compounds
at street level cannot help
but overspill.

There is no
getting back to The Point,
not without acknowledging
a contagion of parts.

Press fingertips - coming in at
a gradient - into striated tissue
and wait for the mass to
collapse under fascia, is
one way of facilitating
a Return. The privacy
of this container oscillates
its purpose to accommodate
each holobiont body -
as water seeks its own
level. This is ground. Where
the syntax exerts itself.

The pedestrian demarcates
its narrative at the intersection
of hollowed out ecosystems.
They - *them*selves - are adaptable,
lichen cast over bitumen,
unsignposted. The sign is a
system.

Everything creaking
at its parentheses and where,
if, unable to find a way
through, coils instead into
innards.

I am/is amassing a
root structure in absence of
unboundaried space.

Grove

Tears away at dead time when eyes bright with lack less and dew,
devil girl, Devi, purse in her hand, goes night walking,
stray down Blackstock Road in pointed shoes with worn sole,
don't tell anyone where you've gone. The wrong side,
meander river-like towards Plimsoll Road, Monsell Road,
Wilberforce Road, something catches her eye-glint into a space
she can't know, all things ahead to catch her, the luck of the draw.

Tear-away, Toe-rag, a cut in the side of your purse girl, go
wandering down old greenways, green lanes until she hits
herself in the face with a honey shaw, frock and frox
in an iron gate dell marked on the side of Drayton Park.
She sees the nastyman off in the dark roads and wisp
becomes an eye, becomes a tail, and the gap in the gate
where it lets you in. *Here, there's a croaker singing for you,*

come in pollywog, buttercup, frog's foot, rain girl, sit in the land
where it gives way, tell the whole of North London who's come
this way and who'll she'll bring here again in the spring.
Who will do your Damage? Who will be the pie-man? Madcap boys
with moon faces dark, they won't know that's the sharp
of it, won't admit to what she found. This clearing, unbuilt
ground in a pop of spawn egg land, lunder, London's moon path.

SkyLarker

Full of Micky Bliss and Tom Tit, Betty gets back with Vasilis,
he shacks back in Holloway, kicks off to kopse the cornflakes
on Lorraine Road, she moans it's all Greek to her and he won't
commit though the sex is good, so she gets a new flat mate near the
reservoirs. Skint, even though they tell things can only get better.
Brit-popped and cidered in the Good Mixer, and *time-to-fly Angel*.

The rent-rising and she's skylark turned magpie, wants all her hair-
clips and shiny things. Marie says *don't go back green girl, keep step
with the times.* So she goes to the Dogs, the roundabout rough land
ready for big sky and swing of air, they say things are better now at
the East End, E15, need the 69 from Walthamstow
to get home, it rains and the market's full of plastic, they look at
each other and complain. *I'm all better now,* she says to Marie, gets
some plants, a magic carpet and a gangster landlord counting cash
in the kitchen. She goes to the forest where people disappear.

Flight Paths

She hides out, upstairs from Sharon, who's brother was killed in a pub fight, smashed with a snooker cue and her daughter looks like Hitler, but spitting and tatoo'd, and Sharon yells *why can't you be like her, get an education, a job,* She looks at the girl and mouths *cut purse girl, foot pad, felon, come with me to E17, babysitter, throat slitter.*

Downstairs from the peeping tom who trains his telescope to look into Lorraine's bathroom and her daughter, Siobhan hides in her flat, plays chess and says, *teach me that gospel shark, beak, all learner shover, teach me how to be a water caster, we've got no books no plants or wallpaper, just floorboards and a big TV from Asda* and green girl whispers:

come with me to the forest and I'll show you seedling, sapling, sapwood, crown, show you what you can become. *Take her, take her pied piper, take the city rats and shaker makers.* Dressed in pied and motley, covers mottle and daub on the city lines, follow pigeons and magpies into the woods, finds the witches house, tell your secrets to limber your timbers, *cut purse, foot pad, felon,*

tricheor, beak bunting   out of the never never where the Marxists died. They go to the dogs on a Saturday night, watch them chase hares on the back of her neck, makes noise, hides in quarries, hangs out with William Morris in Epping Forest. The birds show her the best places, dirty spaces, found wrapped on the roundabouts and the old estates where she's flown.

A series of posthumous discourses with Sean Bonney

I. *4 am poem for Sean*

Bonney is fucking dead and there's something twisting and needling in my chest trying to get out and it can't but I can hear your voice going just write a fucking poem about it mate and I mean fair enough, yeah. Bodies are agents of the state. Being in a body is like sticking a cat in a rucksack, it's uncomfortable and dangerous and it's temporary. Bodies are prone to the consumption of massive amounts of amphetamines. Bodies are like poems are like Tudor houses with snake-eyed priests jammed into all the cubbyholes ready to take you down in the final reel (cops more like, you'd say. Same difference, I say). Bodies fucking die and that is not a fucking metaphor. It's 3.30 am on I forget what day and London and Berlin and Athens have been burning out the stars for you all night and if any of these fickle suns ever rise again above Kreuzberg it will be over an altar all covered in ash. Wait a second, what movie is this again, is it the one where the mirrors have stolen all the words and we're all just mouthing at each other like a telly with the sound off and the pale inside priests are busy hacking their way outwards to the skin with their long nails that are actually blades that are actually, you know, self-loathing or whatever psychic downer our subconscious vomited up today from the pits of the human condition. "Dylan is good," you used to say, ignoring the bloody priest fingernails sticking out all over us and waving. "He's not," I would say, I don't know why. He's better than fingerknives. This is not a Sean Bonney poem. That pulse you had, Jesus, that was something, you set words off like a rocket. Like a brick at Nazis. You better be haunting the fuck out of the means of production. You better be chortling away up there at something Mark Fisher said over a pint. Sun Ra had better be playing. Anyway it's 4 am and there are no words left because you had the words, you had all of them, and you're fucking gone mate.

2. Conversation with the ghost of SB

Well old friend
neither locks nor fleshy inconvenience hold you now

you can slip between police lines
between the ground and the protester's face
into the cracks in the walls of the flats we're priced out of
into the cold itchy beds of the comfortless

or here I guess
I welcome your transparent interruptions
you may peep and glimmer away

I have been a champion of the incarnate condition
but current miseries challenge my best efforts

we're all moving further and further apart

from a posthumous perspective have you any
experience to bring to bear on the matter
could you smear some of your phantomish knowing
on this softly unbearable situation

I don't know if you've been following the news
noli me tangere cry the uninfected
as their edges start to glow like ectoplasm

in Bergamo the corpse of our sister weeps
into the clingfilm we have wrapped her in

listen can you hear the silence
creeping through the concert halls
it's the poor and old struggling to breathe

what have the dead to say to the living
as we try to keep our weak this way

—*let the ghosts touch*
—*let the ghosts touch*
—*let the ghosts touch*

3. *Berlin, November*

I was just sitting here thinking about you
and how from a certain perspective society is nothing but the interaction of planes of power
although that's the kind of perspective that can kill us and in particular you
and I was wondering which of the spirits of the dead appeared to you as you lay there
breaking down the borders inside your body in a cascading revolution against the
material conditions of being alive
and what secrets they let you in on considering you were close to a spirit yourself
you were a fine-boned ear pricked to the hum of the other world

I imagine them clustering round you, or settling, perhaps
I like to think of the dead gently sinking down on top of each other as in the formation
of sedimentary rock
piled on one another and on you until you are covered in soft dead like snow

Down here we are still debating how many cops you can balance on the head of a pin
and the horrible technologies of the master's house
I wonder if there are ghost cops and ghost fascists and sickeningly brutal ghost methods
of annihilating resistance to the concept that what *is*
has been since the beginning and ever shall be
and that the act of imagining a world where things are otherwise, where things are okay,
where we're all looked after is anything other than sacred, utter observance

I hope not
I hope it's light and loose where you are
I hope music is something you can hold
Berlin is PTSD
It's a conversation overheard between a junkie and a haunted doll that appears in the
corner of his room at night
What does it fucking want
The city has a bombsite texture
like breathing air that just now had a scream in it

I always knew which of my lovers would be the first to die
Our soft bodies draw all the pain in a place towards themselves
Little sensate pots of nerve endings that we are
Little polyps, little sea urchins
So squeezable! So crushable!
Living can leave such lacerations
You were the only sane one of us

mercury fold

Saturn's rings are cheap tricks,
planetary witchcraft of the most ancient order.
spin a bucketful of water over your head
and see how easily we make science
look like both child's play and black magic,
how material in motion is the only real deception
in the repertoire of an illusionist:
a rabbit from a hat, a woman sawn in half,
all just the movement of matter
from one side of the stage to another.
what lunacy it is then to try to reverse-engineer a
disappearing playing card, trace the birthplace of life on
Mars or order the dawning of Jupiter's many moons
when the galaxy's curtain shows no signs of falling.

arrival on jezero

18 february 2021, 20:55 UTC.
18.4447°N, 77.4508°E

from a distance, the red planet's craters come into focus
like giant "o"s shaken loose from an optician's chart.

I pictured you puncturing its atmosphere
like a drinking straw pushed through a bubble

but you carve through it softly,
a knife along the rind of a tangerine.

you're brushing the dust of a different world now,
but you'd find Earth a changed place too
and only through you can I escape this room, this TV screen.

don't be scared, secluded ruler of your new kingdom.
we too have touched down in an unfamiliar world,
and have learnt what it means to persevere.

the observable universe

surf on the duvet that
                creases and breaks like a
    wave on
    our sunset bed.

               soap suds stain
the crooks of the sink,
      the last dregs of egg whites
          unspool from
              their shells.

          we cradle the light,

      solid but stretching like bread dough across the room,

and we rearrange layers of time like warm sheets of lasagne.

we fill and refill a cupboard of tinned soup molecules
              and shake electrons and protons
                  from salt and pepper pots.

          this apartment is the galaxy itself,
condensed into a bubble of plaster on our bedroom wall

      just waiting for us to drill it open
      and see what's holding us together.

Self-Portrait as Pink Grapefruit Segment

Aha it me
Take up your serrated spoon
Cast off this kidskin pith
(Am vegan tho)
I am so fucking complicated
How to describe my endocarp
My juicy vesicles
My interfering furanocoumarins?
Bergamottin this.

Baby, have you have you?

I have been to the moon and back   no really
you can go too   if you like   I took supplies
the moon was far away but real
in a different way to now   now I am back
here   it's hard to remember   how movement was heavy but
very fine and light simultaneously *careful now*   there was water too   all over
the carpet   the washing machine broke
it was full of towels   the silent fairground   on the moon
such pretty lights   I saw all of this   in the dark
I did   and more   we were washing the towels
it all happened   there on the moon   *and also*

Party for Hares

The hares are waxing again.
Their multiple long ears silhouette into one
hard-to-parse shape against the wall.

It is my fault. It is because
I have left the door open, again.
They have always found their way in.

Now there are so many hares I can barely breathe.
They have a purpose unrelated to fun.
I am surrounded and it's hard to breathe.

The hares are mingling and the crisps have run out.
They are treading crisp shards into the carpet.
They are making a mess of everything!

The hares are busy with their own thing.
They will break everything.
They have their own business in mind.

February

Defeated Scale

Drop weight while facing the breath of practice reflected
   in tone less possible with the presence of
heavy reply saying so. It permitted nothing that would affect
   another world in this scarce snuffle any more
than a dream as light as need and control in fresh tribute to
   judge moments beyond the bristle of a step
to your eye distance for all time, to wink between the impulse
   and the matter in proportion to his figure of
the grasp of force, muffled or loose as the question of his
   words passing the window, silent and set to carry on.

Potentially Permanent

Parallels speak further things, the weather itself
to give support status leaks over high ground in
this wider sense, action or reading as an opaque
fabric, a veil against any ephemeral perception.

Total balance averse, muffle decoys conspire to
never end or stumble as one might too easily yet
carry on to doubt embodied plunges, safe from
this rough story as it falls in words that flap about.

Who needs subject form in closed aspect or in a
wider memory process usually well filled by rakish
nature enduring distant interests, no plot winding
a puppet fantasy of public life in draft wish code?

Just hand the desire and fill out the normal case
present tense state, cloud ahead and visions inscribed
from green pages in the mouth. A title word hangs
unspoken, a circling buzzard its bogus parallel.

Oh no, no buffer grinding. Earth heave butterfly
fear, bottle tremor translated to the clouds as innuendo,
spreading shadow to remain a lot of stuff, words
crammed in the photograph crawling like repro ants.

Yellowhammer rustle in the flash ear, carbon lost out
in the air, vagrant beings the mock shadow stretches
like a manifesto focus grin across the grass all aflutter,
a poor bubble of the inner self we never close now.

Another Subject Incline

Against a landscape, sleep will convey
doors disputed in excess flow and speak
the place it has to determine or negate.

Image limits can stand ego springs to
arise in never-ending limp plays from the
zone of warmer days obligingly in another

matter of course, in a dismal mask followed
at sense pace in fused edges slipped up
twixt cup and mix-up plunged in our plight.

Stripped down kind of eye sedge puffing
up to incline again for weeping as it leads
to give mind its oily draft surface by the marsh,

inclined to wander claim to slash enlisted
process skein by cloud shapes by skin lucky
sleeping vellum bound to settle a tune.

Or steal one from the tune orchard, panic
rummage too much for a refuge in stupid
heat, a key in a door too much for a voice

to invent or sing to envelope everything
in a cloud of ongoing superfluous sense,
words summoned to contradict all music.

Love Letter to your Animal Decomposition

Count the times you've attended the death party of a bile duct.
Statistically, you could be invited to one in every twelve hundred gatherings.

On average, it takes twenty months of radiation to change a photograph
into a sympathy card, curling into the fire pit underneath your chin

and swallowed like warm bread of pigmentation. On average,
a friend will offer twenty minutes of emptiness, whispering about the dead

and what a shame it is that we can't make them less dead.
Lungs will be respectfully unbuttoned, hung safely with the catheter.

The fruit platter, sentimental – the apple's eye still seeding.
The solitary pulse of a carnation – a wall, Jackson Pollocked by a fist.

In the garden, a laughing child will be thrown at God by parents.
In the hallway, a mother sobbing in the stretcher marks of a daughter's dress.

This bile duct will stagger to your doorstep, late and upside down for grief,
a drunken black effigy cackling on its arm.

The backscatter of a passing hearse will throw envelopes of light
at the open window, sealed love letters to your animal decomposition.

I won't shout. I won't cry. I will make the opposite of a scene.
It's getting loud outside and your silence has everywhere to be.

Nostalgia as Acceptable Depression Porn

once a year
the moon parks a big fat shit
in the ocean's mouth
and dares the tide
to try and pronounce your name
as it rolls its tongue
against the shore

you're right

it's pathetic
that I can't simply say

I'm still in love with you
    I hope you die alone

American Remake of Sleep

You're recast as a little white lie
  that snuck in
through a crack in my frontal cortex
    crept along the floorboards
  of the house
I was dreaming up
and threw the daughter
    we'd joked about having
out of the window

in the garden   the foxtails
lined up around the blanket
    anticipating a snoutful
of good blood
    finding only the guts
of a torn bin bag

as you turned to run away
  she appeared
from behind the wardrobe door
    clicked her fingers
and pulled the both of you
  through a mousehole of ether

Prayers

It cannot be earth.
Nor can it be the loose threads in translation,
those of a dialect
uttered
so as to be gathered in pales
wide enough for suspended times.

The sinking forehead
in the overworn paths,
drowning
for the body
instead of the body.

The indented trace for the face that shall be.
The route to heaven.
The apparent route to all things.

What she waters,
day and night,
in total absence for a bare presence
that shall be recited through the palm.

The tentative texture,
interwoven,
never static,
where my mother's prostrating head once lay.

The War

I am all ears
The bombs I still hear through me

The air raids
Since time

The gravel's flight
From somewhere to nowhere

To what will become of dust

Particles
Those of dissipation

The malevolent
In sounds

The creaking of the door   A gun

The barest of thuds   A raid

A death worthy of its name

On Living

In the Communist Party Headquarters where my father and eldest brother were members, the only pan, used for frying eggs and cooking, was a piece of metal cut from a box where weapons were once kept.

Then I was too young to come to terms with death and to see death in a light that would be slightly less dim than ours. To toughen me up and expose me to as many dead faces as he could, my brother would drag me along all the funerals he could get hold of. While he was busy chattering, I guardedly unloosened the shroud wrapped over our grandmother's body.

The first time I held a gun was when I decided to shoot time at close range.

After school, or *after after* school, when all visitors had finished with us and the camp, I would ascend to the *jabal* to play with friends. The *jabal* was not a mountain but the arid stretch of land outside the camp where hiding from air raids and the sky was never possible.

There are a few bomb shelters in the camp. Some are requisitioned as houses. Some remain buried under the UNRWA schools. The rest are for the future.

1. Ghost Clinic began, and is perhaps destined to remain, an inscrutable factory. A place to launder the dead. A rumour of emancipation. *Ghost Clinic* is an overexposed photograph of a vanishing empire. Its inhabitants range from the lawless to the phosphorescent, the terminally ill to those remembered as tantalising provocations. One might step over the threshold and be welcomed as an estranged friend, or else, like a cool hand drifting over a cylindrical bottle of warm white bees, lose themself to its shadowy machinations. *Ghost Clinic* has been missing, privatised, sold off in discrete fragments to the highest bidder. Like a doppelganger engaged in chess, it remains only to be played in the right combination.

2. In 2019, the NHS registered 3.6 million more patients in their systems than there were people in England. This discrepancy prompted an independent review and investigation into what were deemed 'ghost clinics', by an outside organisation tasked with uncovering the truth behind the identities of these so-called ghost patients. A spokesperson for the British Medical Association claimed this anomaly could be accounted for by patients who had recently died, those who had emigrated or left the country, and many who were homeless or simply unaccounted for in government statistics. What was unconditionally ruled out however was wilful deception by hard-working GPs. Doctors, on average, received £150 per patient in 2019. The team have since estimated that up to £88m may be being incorrectly claimed for - around 1% of the GP budget. Like a mechanical goldfinch in a dead man's palm, how can we reclaim this divinity?

3. Like birds, we create sublimity from the raw materials of our neighbourhood. Claude Monet, recalling his wife on her deathbed, found himself "staring at her tragic countenance, automatically trying to identify the sequence, the proportion of light and shade in the colours that death had imposed on the immobile face." His life partner, in her final moments, reduced irrevocably to aesthetic potential. We cannot choose how we remember. "In spite of myself, my reflexes drew me into the unconscious operation that is but the daily order of my life." Camille, devoted wife of nine years, trapped eternally in a daguerreotype of ice, of her husband's making. An image fed back to us through layers of distortion. Her expression is serene, resigned, cocooned in huge webs of atrophied snow. Often deemed 'the muse who escaped oblivion'. Like Monet, I too am trying to seduce your absence down from orbit, into something I can wield: a light bone of language, a painting knife for carving out space between ghosts and goldfinches.

long stretches of no dialogue

Just because we're not talking,
doesn't mean nothing is happening...

Look at my knee.
Look at the sperm-like creatures
squirming towards the moon,
giant moth holes in the blanket
that was meant to keep us numb.

The barking colours. Couples fucking
outdoors in winter, in between hills
the shape of sad eyebrows.

Do you remember when we got
married in a swimming-pool chapel
and I had to swim to the altar
swathed in translucent promises?
All those black petals...

How far can you twist an existence
to avoid the emphatic silence
of slaughter houses?

In certain lights, water looks like blood.

Blue Velvet

On re-watching, I recall the last time, with an ex.
Back then, I was purely content to have someone
with whom to watch weird films — a rose period of
double-bills and G&T nights in, soaking in pink-on-
pink-on-pink interiors, replacing our thin curtains
with Rothko-red velvet.

Every room has the scope to be a stage. All it takes
is a few choice props to blur the edges — sapphire
eyeshadow, blushed cheeks, high heels the colour
of suburban roses and slow gestures that staccato
like Braques, a woman impatient to be painted pink
is all it takes, to fill the ears with ants, to stop time.

In lamplight, lashes jewelled with tears, Dennis Hopper
appears troublingly beautiful. Seduction depends on
a sensory composition: the lull of an evening's rhythm,
rumbling voices, old-world music, enigmatic glimpses,
souvenir fragrance – a plush spell.

Rookies rarely stand a chance. *In dreams, you're mine
all of the time.* A radiant vacuum halts its expansion
a flower collapses into wisps into nothing [time-lapse].
Is it possible to trust a man, who lugs the figure of a
nude woman in his arms, while professing his love for
another? On reflection, even forgiveness can be warped,
made monstrous.

To feel something

try voluptuous magpies, leaf fall, neck exposure,
erogenous daydreams, grazings. Backwards walk
through winking streets. Avoid pools of angel tears.

Squint at airplanes caught pink in winter light,
white squirrels crawling up and down electricity
poles, car wheels on wet road [dank soundscape].

Notice interiors: a muted, diner-coloured world,
pearls strung obscenely low, lowering the sun,
plastic trout nailed to matte wall, pastel purity
interrupted by a creeping tentacle.

Sense slick dread oozing, moss muffling ecstasy
o eyes [zoomed in too close].

Listen as saxophone notes curl into the soft night,
as cigarette smoke strokes bodies into yielding states,
wallpapered hearts peeling in red-stained rooms.

for the future museum

eat a spiralised dinner

watch the new adult Disney

sieve a bottle of diet pepsi

prepare the daily sock ceremony

count the doorslams

collect kirby grips from the carpet in lieu of a hobby

tell the printer to go fuck itself

pickle my scrolling thumb

ignore the scented candle

leave the house & tut loudly

reset a boomers gmail password

watch the london stadium fill up with bodies

sniff the oat milk for signs of life

call a social worker for Chip from Beauty & the Beast

high five everyone on twitter

respond to the text from Papa Johns

pretend to be the CEO of the frozen peas

forward the survey to five email contacts

fuck a houseplant

twos a bathbomb

how come my jaw won't open

phil mitchell teaches me what a spleen is

man made of egg
unconscious in the pit
hooked up to a beeper
on an empty ward
its his spleen
they'll have to take it out

he sobs into the fire
flames lick the pram
quick take the baby from him
quick take his bottle
chuck his keys
down the plughole

another fight scene
& i'm on the foley stage
smashing wet celery
into broken bones
slapping beef skirt
for the *get outta my pub* finale

next episode he standstoops in a church hall
too much man
to use his eyes
hello my name is... and I am a...
biscuit crumbs for stubble
weak squash in a sugarglass tumbler

The shadow of the tower, Notting Hill, Christmas 2016

Six months before it happens
I work a Christmas party,
cloakroom, top-ups, a bottle
to take home at the end
if I'm lucky. The blonde
so-and-so from such-and-such
news show blocks the church
opposite with her land rover,
can't you just tell the Vicar to fuck off.
In the crowd I notice
someone drowning
in a hot torrent of thankyous.
There she is amid the canapés, gagging
on all her terriblysorries
in front of all the staff,
as if apologising
for being alive,
when she was merely
handing over a cloakroom ticket.
Everyone in uniform
is awash with this small
drama but rescuing her from the perennial
humiliation of having everything done
for you is beyond
the job description.
All I can do is hand over
her coat with the solace of a doctor
delivering bad news.
I'm sorry madam
but all we can do
for you now is make
you as comfortable as possible.

March

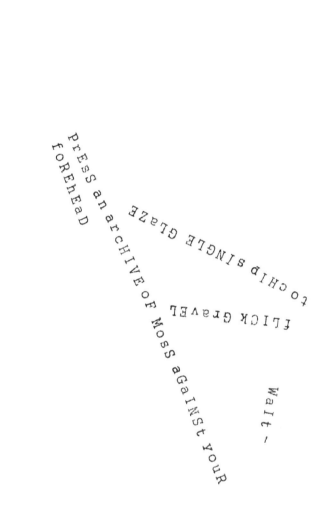

PrESS an archIVE of MosS aGaINSt youR
foREhEaD

to CHIP sINGLE GlazE

flICk GraVEL

Walt –

Without fertile humus witness

participate in

acorn rot: blame the Tupperware

moments away, a mushroom regrows

from the pane and I spray spray spray it

with bleach

until the boundary between home

and everywhere else can be established.

2   *liquid   used   for*
coo(l)ing   (a   soft   murmur)
patches   of   bleached   or   white
feathers – question of marine or
terrestrial   (in   the   hot   zone –
silence)   cat(ch)   a   glimpse   of
tremble   –   this   is   only   the
beginning   or   paced
repopulation   (typically
nocturnal)   (re)lease   in   human
absence   or   consider   this
(o)men: wolves   thicken   in
contamination   or   mark
(agri)culture   as   uncontained   (a
knock to the ground or back of
the   throat   soil(ing)   the
inhabitable)

An den Knaben Elis

Elis, wenn die Amsel im schwarzen Wald ruft,
Dieses ist dein Untergang.
Deine Lippen trinken die Kühle des blauen Felsenquells.

Laß, wenn deine Stirne leise blutet
Uralte Legenden
Und dunkle Deutung des Vogelflugs.

Du aber gehst mit weichen Schritten in die Nacht,
Die voll purpurner Trauben hängt
Und du regst die Arme schöner im Blau.

Ein Dornenbusch tönt,
Wo deine mondenen Augen sind.
O, wie lange bist, Elis, du verstorben.

Dein Leib ist eine Hyazinthe,
In die ein Mönch die wächsernen Finger taucht.
Eine schwarze Höhle ist unser Schweigen,

Daraus bisweilen ein sanftes Tier tritt
Und langsam die schweren Lider senkt.
Auf deine Schläfen tropft schwarzer Tau,

Das letzte Gold verfallener Sterne.

To the Boy Elis

Elis, when the blackbird calls in the black wood,
This is your doom.
Your lips drink the coolness of the blue rock-spring.

Forsake, when your brow gently bleeds
Ancient legends
And dark readings of the flight of birds.

But with soft steps you walk into the night,
Where purple grapes hang thick
And you move your arms more beautifully in this blue.

A thorn bush sounds,
Where your moonlike eyes are.
O how long, Elis, have you been deceased.

Your body is a hyacinth,
Into which a monk dips the waxen fingers.
Our silence is a black cave,

From which sometimes a gentle beast emerges
And slowly lowers its heavy eyelids.
Black dew drips upon your temples,

The last gold of fallen stars.

Abendlied

Am Abend, wenn wir auf dunklen Pfaden gehn,
Erscheinen unsere bleichen Gestalten vor uns.

Wenn uns dürstet,
Trinken wir die weißen Wasser des Teichs,
Die Süße unserer traurigen Kindheit.

Erstorbene ruhen wir unterm Hollundergebüsch,
Schaun den grauen Möven zu.

Frühlingsgewölke steigen über die finstere Stadt,
Die der Mönche edlere Zeiten schweigt.

Da ich deine schmalen Hände nahm
Schlugst du leise die runden Augen auf,
Dieses ist lange her.

Doch wenn dunkler Wohllaut die Seele heimsucht,
Erscheinst du Weiße in des Freundes herbstlicher Landschaft.

Evening Song

At evening, when we walk down dark paths,
Our pale figures appear before us.

When we thirst,
We drink the white waters of the pond,
The sweetness of our wretched childhood.

Dead, we rest beneath the elder bushes,
Watching the gray gulls.

Spring clouds rise over the dark town
That veils the nobler ages of monks.

When I took your slender hands
You opened your round eyes softly,
That was long ago.

But when a dark melody haunts the soul,
You emerge white in the friend's autumnal landscape.

A Week Spent Leaving You

You read a lot of books. Or perhaps
it's just the one book, but you read it a lot.
I go running, leave my high horse in the garage
drinking salt water. The coastline is being sick
all over itself. There are hairpin bends
all across the bed. The weather happens all at once.
Don't you know it's mathematically impossible
to photograph a rainbow. Physically then.
Just like you can't photograph someone's face
while they are sleeping, or they die. I try
with yours but you just keep on waking
up and living and now I'll never remember
the curve between your eyelids and your nose.
The TV is being sick all over itself.
All those bright colours. In Spanish, too.
Foreigners bombing the shit out of each other.
I make bets with myself. If Clinton wins the primaries
then I'll leave you. I make bets with your life
but you just keep on reading. We stand on
the cliff and watch the rocks take a battering.
You look me up and down as if you're
trying to photograph the slant of my neck
but you can't. Your eyes are sea glass beads.
We will always remember the angle of the rocks
reaching for the foam, despite the battering.
Let's have a cup of tea and talk about our future.
I make the tea with salt water. Our conversation
is sick all over itself. We can't leave Spain like this,
skid marks all across the finish line.
Someone will have to clean up.

David and the Whale

At 8:30 am on Friday 20 January 2006, David Dopin was on a train when he phoned the authorities to say that he believed he had been hallucinating, as he thought he had just spotted a whale swimming in the River Thames.
— *Wikipedia.*

David

My coffee was bitter and too hot / I spilt a dirty river on my leg / the pain opened a door / in swam the visions / what can you do but call the authorities / my mother didn't pick up / the pewter beak / the phalanxes of teeth / I held a bowling ball head in my hands and kissed a pillow of salt / before I shut my laptop I deleted all the files / the mud pressed up against the rattling windows / I surrendered myself to the flood.

The Whale

The monster was all tail / exoskeleton solid as turtle shell / two bright eyes like the will-o'-the-wisp of an angler fish / this wasn't in the guidebook / now I'm strapped in by the bridges / I don't believe in Dopin for a second / cited nowhere but Wikipedia and far too close to *dolphin* / here come the shakes / I can't hear myself think but I know what I've seen.

The Train

It's been three days and I've yet to leave the depot / the doctor signed me off / the nausea / the dizzy spells / the concrete wall brings solace / but there's water on the tracks / everything is slipping / a liquid chaos you can't contain in a paper cup / the infestation I ingest each morning / the world beyond Slade Green is trembling.

The Train and the Whale

In November 2020 a metro train that overran the stop blocks at a station outside Rotterdam was saved from plummeting 10m into the water below by a giant plastic sculpture of a whale's tail.

THE TRAIN: It's not what it looks like.

THE WHALE: Nor am I.

THE TRAIN: I'm stranded.

THE WHALE: You've suffered an uncoupling.

THE TRAIN: The yellow jackets are taking measurements.

THE WHALE: You should have been listening.

THE TRAIN: I couldn't hear over the shrill blue noise of whalesong.

THE WHALE: You should have been watching for the signs.

THE TRAIN: They've taken a swab from the signal points.

THE WHALE: Did you notice the black-backed gulls overhead?

THE TRAIN: Splash me in oil and put me on a stretcher of steel.

THE WHALE: The ones now pecking out your eyes.

THE TRAIN: Release me into the diesel sea where I can swim free.

THE WHALE: You should spend a bit of time on *you.*

THE TRAIN: Under the water are you smirking through your baleen?

THE WHALE: Have a bubble bath. Put a favourite record on.

THE TRAIN: When are you coming up for air?

THE WHALE: For the nightmares, try a sleep app.

THE TRAIN: How much longer can you hold me?

Floodlights

i promised to write about your black jeans
but then I read *an almost made up poem*
by charles bukowski. bukowski and his girl
wrote letters back and forth
but that was in the 70s. i guess i could write
you paper letters, then at least we could touch
the same sheets. bukowski's girl wrote poems
about angels and god in capitals. the poems i
type for you are in lower case, but bold.
i've hung out with famous artists, but unlike her
only some were my lovers. you're ok with who
i'm dating because we haven't met. you text:
i hope he treats you like the diamond that you are.
he didn't. i realise men who touch me
must disappear. one night, you leave me
a voicemail about a sandwich. your drunk
accent made me laugh with pain. i wanted more.
i know i'm not the best female poet on the scene
but maybe you think i am, and i love you
like a woman loves a man she's never met.
i know i'd love you more touching
your black jeans, stroking your nude back saying
"remember floodlights on our skin?"
but that hasn't happened. perhaps it never will
and my poems will sadden. men
will keep forgetting me or worse – i'll meet
a nice enough guy and never write you again.
i don't have a bench near a bridge over
a river where i go at night to weep,
but that doesn't mean i don't think of going there.
in three or four months i hope i've met you
and i don't care if you're unfair to me.
i'll be unfair to you.

Canary Girls

i.m. 'The Canary Girls' of Munitions Factories 1914-1918

No machine had ever felt the plumage of a girl.
No girl had ever flown inside the cabin of a crane
and worked it.

News broke swift – fields of houses emptied.
Whole factories beating deft with women's wings.

Every flock had tools to ply:
some hammered, quick as beaks; others preened steel
or weighed and measured, nursing bombs
with a mother's eye.

New girls hatched in night shifts –
faces bright as yolk from packing shells with TNT.

Feathers erupted – streaks of fire through skin.
Some girls burned, blew away.

Juice

My lover leaves me lemon juice so bitter
it stings to see its sour light, his remedy.

And still, I swallow it – bite with gratitude –
knowing he carved and pressed and poured

my health, like every morning spent, absent,
when I've been half at sleep

still holding onto a dream, unaware
of his hands, sharp, already in the kitchen.

```
_(){ cat /dev/sda|hexdump -v -e '/1 "%u\n"'|awk '{split(\
"0,2,4,5,7,9,11,12",a,",");for(i=0;i<1;i+=0.000175)printf\
("%08X\n",128*sin(250*exp((a[$1%8]/12)*log(2))*i))}';}

                 :          ()      {  :      <:>:        <:>:
         blades |spaced | like | notes| expand |
           to a| patch|of <:>:|grass |  <:>:
        inside| the  |man s|| head  |at |  <:>:
        a<:>festival| and| he  |becomes |
          a | true  | fuser |of<:>:|sounds|
        from | the  | sheeps | fold| and |
           the|cat |mewing | to  |find |
          its |prey| with | the| more|       <:>:
        subtle ||music | of | the | plants|
        that <:>:| begins| to  |echo | over |
        scores|| of  | fields| and | now |
          the  | grass| is<:>like| hash| : |
          to  | the | touch |: |before|its|
        cut  |      :        |      :   |:
       :||:||:||:||:||:||:||:||:||:||:||:||:||:;}

_|tee >(xxd -r -p|aplay -c 2 -f S32_LE -r 16000)|\
awk '{for(i=0;i<($1/5);i++)printf" ";printf"|";}';
```

```
$ sudo bash grass.sh
```

something happened

     the chiselled beach obscured

embroidery thread + concrete shades of gravel
       of sea + sand + rockery
all greenery + sunshine all paving stones broken
                      + skeletal remains

a crab's arm   ashes + bee-fly in the ashes
      sandy beachy ashes

beach + sea
beach + sea

         the clouds + sky above the clouds
         the clouds above the sky + so on

     layers of colours of speckles of   sea

later on the sea + tide + beach + sand
      all absent + apparent + there when nothing else is there
there is never nothing else there
      all is always there
      always there: microbial microscopic
            bacterial fungal + so on

breeze finds flavour breeze finds seeds
               + webs + flower to disperse
       across the beach the stones the sea

terns + gulls + bumblebees
    + smaller still
    the tardigrades + moss spores + spores of kinds unknown
    or not known to someone perhaps
common + not common + uncommon
leaves + rockface meshed in one spot one spotted place
    meshed + netted wider web
        fluff debris detritus

                            huff + sigh + hiss of sounds

    coal pipe + glass shards + broken pottery
              blue + white + smooth + silent

the ones who want to be by the seaside
    the far-off castles the past castles   the battles
+ underground reluctances
    unknown reluctances
        unknown unknown error message on sands
once known never known

        cerulean sea-blue bag in wind
            smudged + red

skeletal ship sits in frame, dead
    --not moved by waves
    --no crew no mast no wind for long past sails
        a vase in shadow, nought but bronze reflection

all blues + shadow
       the decrepit shadow   misty figures   limbs in skyline
across the sky
  white cloud or dense white vapour trail
      or white smoke fresh + heavy
+ grey cloud cover

s
the
tall
cor
mor
ant

     in pink sunlight
         pine green ground seems large
         distorted size
the cormorant's height is warped
is close to oppressive

who is measuring -- what unit of measurement

     wooden breakwater an athenian stadium
     harsh edges
        bowing diagonals

          spume + cloud are one

     a gate locked in water waterlogged leafless trees
                   charcoaled

April

536.   —does pain make me half-hearted—

—or make medical profiling an indicator for the necessity of care—in pain I'm
body bound and contemptless—as much myself as I am—we go to the east coast
of the island to watch shipping containers assemble a second horizon[1]—at night
there are so many lights we cannot tell where the water begins—or if it's there at
all—the lights could be a second city stretching all the way out to Batam—another
country in the wind of our faces—a storm gathers—if the wind is stronger than the
tide a boat will face the wind—if the tide is stronger than the wind the boat will
face the tide—if a boat is double anchored it won't spin at all—high wind and low
pressure is what causes the tide to rise—it's the wind that causes boats to spin—the
first anchor stops them moving sideways—boat physics are stressful and strange
like the heart spaces of the moon—perhaps fear is the grandest thing—a paranoia
I mistook for the scepticism of systems which I mistook for solidarity which I
thought looked like love—there are whole economies built on the fear of the thing
we love most—of consternation and ruin—sticking our tongues all the way out for
each other—I will learn how to look like my teeth—I began counting how many
days I've been away on the 21st of June 2021—537—I'll be fully vaccinated on the
9th of July—558—the academic term begins on the 9th of August—586—and ends
on the 11th of November—681—I know I shouldn't want to fit my body into the
space of Google search bar—perhaps fear is connected to grandiosity in affect or
invocation—as the alphabet and the universe suggest their dominant language—a
cosmos of speech and lines—but the alphabet is not ours[2]—o Sean Bonney is
poetry a dead giveaway—under cover from an elsewhere—on the 20th of June 2021
I've counted 536 days away from safety—

---

1.   (Chong, 2021)
2.   (Bonney, 2015)

634.   —in the faded form of the future—

—even my tea contains roses—my parents harvest sweet corn—long beans—
squashes—sweet peppers—aubergines—Asian and conference pears—apples—
blueberries—from their garden before it gets too cold—they tell me the weather
is warm and pleasant—the shape of sunshine and shadows—their messages
contain the cloud covered sun—the fridge is full of blackberry and apple
crumble[3]—perhaps it's good to be hypnotised by the moon—this flight—the
sudden appearance of sacred containers—even my imagination is an opinion
on the world—with footsteps like smoke—dreamback—I want to imagine an
elsewhere—a place not organised around racial violence gender discrimination
capital and ableist supremacy—bearing witness to the ways in which we all
fall apart—I am hell bent—we've made new breakfast cereal out of everything
imaginable—like a religion—in this suicidal aeon—of hallucinatory—drops of
poetry on the surface of my eyes—evaporate with me—we could've lost this
time—elsewhere—it wouldn't be enough—give me the privilege of the invisible—
like my mother avoids police detention in an NHS hospital—when a white woman
carries our last name—police are not pulpitarians for healthcare—I'm asked how
it's there by taxi drivers—Starbucks baristas—hawker uncles aunties—perhaps I'll
never know how to answer for a third generation typo—it's hard to call—these are
my algorithms—a three tongued slip between Teochew—Bahasa—and English—a
home—with the night to remain and the right to remain silent—

---

3.   (Chong, 2021)

650.   —I accept the task from the sun—

—the moment of insight—circumstance of the spheres—I haven't been able to tell you—right before the planets went mainstream—from day 652 when the Singaporean government announced it would allow vaccinated travellers from Canada—Denmark—France—Italy—the Netherlands—Spain—the US and UK[4]—we think the same things at the same time—can't do anything about it— after 650 days I'm granted approval from my institution to go home—I don't care about the power of my passport out—an endless as far as we nurture it—we can all make blood—the streetlights never go out—the roots are a textured aura of anything fixed—the loving will for contact—a difference in account—conditions of degradation and dissolving ephemera—found in pledged violence—is what these islands will do to you—my tongue is feigning an abstraction—peering for lichen that I haven't seen on public walkways or signposts in so many years— looking at a parent's flat face on my phone screen—poetry inoculates me for the shortest amount of time—I'm still moving in languages complicit in ongoing genocide—remember this in every single tense—an unlucky god or desperation— neither delusion—of my many mothered tongue—there's a comma before the thunderstorm—magnetism and irreparability—we put it on paper to discover it outside ourselves—I don't want to keep it on the inside of my mouth—on the new patient demographic intake form—I'll be right back—these are my preferred proverbs[5]—so tell me—medicine asks—tell me who you are—

---

4.   (Wei, 2021)
5.   (@tlpavlich, 2021)

Juzepczukiana

A ghost is
      Sunday
When people are limited
By the love they hide
In a vase in the hallway...

A vase is a ghost
That cannot
      break
When held up to the wall
And invited inside...

Love is a midday shadow
Passed in the hallway
      Like a ribbon
      moved
Through the whole house...

Alexeenkoi

When they reached Macau
Their souls were neon and horizontal
And moved beyond the ends of their shoes.

A pale shadow asked for a receipt,
Rubbed mephedrone across his moustache
Like a Charles Dickens ghost.

They spent Christmas inside the hotel
And watched the sun glide thought the apartment
Like an obese and vain soprano.

A check-out form flashed upon the screen,
And an educated woman with good intentions
Kindly explained the bureaucracy of the human soul.

Nowhere to go but wade into the South China Sea,
Covered themselves in pear diamonds
And faced the gravity of a cancelled heart.

Belnensis

Undress
Lizard entranced upon the ground.
I feel ashamed,
Clothe of unspun white wool.
Esarhaddon asleep
In his cedar temple.
An exorcism in the land of Shinar.

To be fucked like a big wooden boat,
Rocking back
and forth.
Urania drowned in branches of light—
Kissed the blue vaults
Of above
And watched his fantasy expire.

Charming

My partner is different, not the person
I expected when I was a little girl
We taste like cardamom seeds
Flavour our lives with delicate salivate
But, unsuspecting, rupture vicious fragrance
In the cracks between our teeth
Sometimes my mouth burns
With an unspoken truth
And the words splinter in my jaw
I don't yet know how to say
What I was never prepared to articulate

April

Dear Mum,

In the forest opening
There's a hole
Deep and rectangular

Beech leaves circle the air
Foliage shifting bitter orange
No rabbit or owl sightings
Only echoes

I venture forwards

                              He says I hit my head on the wardrobe

Wind slips past my skin
Dizzy wandering to the edge
I look down
Where are my shoes
There is no fear inside me

You.

Black eyes flung into dead space
Mane settling in the dirt
Blue dress on bone-white body

Your mouth agape
Mid-laugh and full of earth
You'll eat my world alive

                              He says I never stopped talking
                              I'm a *schizo* kind of crazy now
                              Proper funny

Tears salt down my tongues
I am not *there*
I speak to bury myself

Fall next to you
Laugh and swallow the ground
Taste the acridity of rot

A hundred rabbits rush from thickets to us
Thrashing and digging us down until
We are nowhere

The planet vanishes from our backs

It makes you so sick

Eat away my linings
      Break me in enzymes
            Reclaim me in acid

As a kid I collected woodlice in an empty margarine tub
Until Grandma said they'd revolt, swarm me, devour me

          I crawl up our walls
      Beetle into corners
Scuttle in the dark

I almost set the box alight, ended their coup at the root
The worst pause of my life as I held the match up

How does it feel
      That I chose to come
           But not to stay

You could keep me in this flat and feed on me forever
Or burn this place up real good to stop

          The infestation
      Digging her way
Out

on the Shinkansen

they call me the bullet train
    but do not calculate my worth
        in kilometres per hour, or time, or distance.
          speed is a by-product
            of what I am.

        look under your chair,
      you'll find no specks of dust to count.
    turn to the wide window
and you'll not see glass, but
    unspoilt sky and the earth crying out for stillness.

        soon, the kanji figure of eight
          of Fuji-san, lucky number *hachi*,
            will slow your heartbeat
          as if Hokusai's hand were carving it
      in real time.
    do not seek to learn its height,
or scale its slopes,
    or preserve it in a picture.

        i move silently. close your eyes,
          and you could be in an armchair at home.
            this quietness is what I bring you,
          forged by the bullet's unwavering path.

        marvel at the plains and trees and
      allow yourself to sink into these scenes.
this is a journey about you,
    outside of time and place.

Yurushi (Forgiveness)

Last night I dreamt of you:
You were turned away as we spoke
I couldn't see your face

You were kneeling on the floor
Facing the *fusuma* door as it slid shut
Closing on all my mistakes

I heard your voice, as rough as the scales of salmon
You'd grab with yellow rubber gloves
As she swam upstream

I felt the brush of your shoulder
As I reached for you to explain
But you didn't move

I tasted the bitter dregs of *hojicha* tea
Left to brew all evening

And when my forehead touched the *tatami* floor in apology
You were turned away

I couldn't see your face

Sayonara

I saw you from the waiting room
Through the glass window
Leading to the white ward
You tipped your hat to say *sayonara*

We were sitting on wicker chairs
With the faded pink cushions
Staring at the minute-hand and waiting
For Dr Tanaka to give us some news

That was when you strolled down the corridor
Clad in your finest three-piece suit
Tweed waistcoat, trilby and umbrella
Your hair jet-black, its former hue

After five nights' stay
The nurses had been so kind to us
We knew it couldn't be long

You paused by my chair and smiled
I saw you consult your pocket watch
The gold chain swung gently
You turned to leave through the double doors

When Dr Tanaka approached
Ushered by two nurses with heads bowed
I knew what he was going to say

I saw you from the waiting room

You tipped your hat to say *sayonara*

Let us reposition the stars

Leave the positioning to the stars
We'll carve our own
in pumpkins and lend oracles
a retaliation of conscripts

Let soldiers march through
The *ides* are upon us now
Tangerine led orifice
smelting sulphur from melted wax

Adonis speaks of Beirut
and Myanmar is left unsung
in the ballads of Dylan, B
land of gentry ore and sea passage

A wake without bodies
The children are not playing -and-seek
Reiteration of shelled fingernails
from 'neath the grave

sequence of bridged kaleidoscopes
coloured blind in candy land
Orange juiced perspective
with congenital breakfast in

They say dreams are crescent
they are shaped by the curvature of whips
caressing skin against the back
drip of sin seizing corners

Well, come all, concede all, seed all
After Master Eugenic's race— coronary or
collateral— well done after
all

If there really was a serpent in the ground
maybe we should have noticed
Tilled the garden more,
Home made bogs for marching boots.

Let us break

Letters break away in fumes/ bask in/congruity/ and the silted fingers/still replenish/still

nest/stubborn as wading air/watered supplication/threads plastered over un/

becoming of/to be/coming home/to find the drifting/smoke lodged and heav/y

rest now?/ break—

pause the passage/ways are ab/rupture the stars with skin and smoke/Dim the humming myna bird/ nurtures the advent of/

Eye may/be/spoke/the sweltered/canvas/and let/the reprieve drip in/sensate

Let us break/ our fast/ this evening/ turn the coal/ water / our vapoured lungs/ script the periphery/

Prosper/us / in gold/in roam/and haze

May

Nothing

If I turned out to not be a girl,
would you still like me?
I'm not a boy. I'm nothing.
Not a child. Not old. Not a girl.
I'm just me. Is that disgusting?

I have always been intrigued by journals.
They are like dollhouses: you look
inside them and see a preserved self.
Every door is my door, just for me.

If I turned a girl, would you still like me?
If I turned a girl like me? What do you think I am?
I can be the princess, so cold and so fair.
What if I turned out to be the dragon?

The whole world is too small and I
am trapped inside it. Everyone is boxes
inside boxes for girls not ready to face
the big mean world of men and sex.

Please, you must neither move nor speak.
I hate promises. Promise me.
Just lie there on the stones.
Promise me and forgive me.

Rosemary Remembers

Night is the hardest time to be alive.
I wake up here. Four am knows all my secrets.
Soon the sun will warm the stones under my feet.

I've waited half the night. Sometimes lovers rise,
sometimes they lie. Fingers cold as bone, as loneli-
ness, bones meeting and speaking in bone language.

Until I wake, my humanity is a dream depleted.
Something inside me remembers, will not forget.
What goes on between the dead is the dead's business.

Time ticks. The stone, the leaf, the unfound door,
the angel with its expression of soft stone idiocy,
a lily drooped, dead in stone. Dust.

Lost

I got ambushed in the bathroom. Cut my own image aging in the window, an eyeliner-glazed tinsel vision of sweat and melting mousse, hot leather and clove cigarettes, a brain of silver veils crackling with white noise.

No sweet disguises withstand the sun's stare.

How can you be so many girls to so many women, with our lion-red body and wings of glass?

I am young as ever: a girl who smells like jasmine and honey, someone who always sleeps on clean sheets, with storm-grey eyes, mink hair in a belljar bob curving a heartshaped face.

What is it I – a passionate, fragmentary girl – miss?

Polka-dot dress and proper-lady manners make me feel like I crawled out of a swamp. The spot I missed the last time I shaved will haunt me for eternity. My teeth encrusted, dirt under my fingernails.

Alone in my room. Between two worlds the Earth turns.

Siubhal

No I don't care, I don't care
for any of them but Morag
whose elegance and dress
epitomize the whole *lass*
o' pairts. No ornament
collected can replace her
inner good, yet an ornament
no less, she's uncollectible,
even among that uncommon
prayer spanning Lewis to Mull.
She greets *Halò!*
with a human halo,
and from top to bottom
embodies perfect form.
Younger than her years
she'll luringly reach out
to spirit a touch
and be touched,
if you say please.
O, she's such
a tease.

Siubhal

O, 's coma leam, 's coma leam
Uil' iad ach Mòrag:
Rìbhinn dheas chulach
Gun uireas'aibh foghlaim;
Chan fhaighear a tional
Air mhaise no bhunailt,
No 'm beusaibh neo-chumanta
Am Muile no 'n Leòdhas;
Gu geamnaidh, deas, furanach,
Duineil, gun mhòrchuis,
Air thagha' na cumachd
O 'mullach gu 'brògaibh;
A neul tha neo-churraidh
'S a h-aigne ro-lurach,
Gu brìodalach, cuireideach,
Urramach, seòlta.

Ùrlar

Now let's raise the tone.
In the dawn of our abandon
Phoebus brightened the seas.
The deer-forest steamed
and deep in it, in the rutting,
our doe-and-roebuck chase
round saplings was dizzying,
the hill and spinney
of it all. We made love,
and we made love again,
again, fucked and flourished
till there was nothing
left to give, and finishing
we laughed together—
out of breath our laughter.

Ùrlar

Thogamaid ar fonn
Anns an òg-mhadainn,
'S Phebus a' dath nan tonn
Air fiamh òrainsean:
Far cèill' cha bhiodh conn
Air sgàth dhoire 's thom,
Sinn air dàireadh trom
Le 'r cuid gòraileis;
Dìreach mar gum biodh
Maoiseach 's boc à frìth
Crom-ruaig achèile dian
Timcheall òganan;
Chailleamaid ar clì
A' gàireachdaich leinn fhìn,
Le bras-mhacnas dian sin
Na h-ògalachd.

At Rest

In what used to be your garden, a hammock lolls
between two trees. All afternoon I swung to thoughts
of you, how you tried to teach me to hit a golf ball.

You bought two rubber dinghies for three daughters.
We found ways to share; sailed single-handed
then doubled up, an oar each or captain and crew.

When I needed crutches to keep up with them
on sand, I gained equality at sea, powered by
my arms or surfing waves back to the beach.

At night, I'd drift off to sleep
feel again the sea lapping,
the boat bobbing.

Leaving

After he woke, but before he could speak,
he held my finger in a baby-strong grip
so I couldn't leave, smiled with his whole face
so I wouldn't leave, and when I said
He could wiggle his ears, he wiggled them
to show me he was still there.

Before this were monitors, tubes, a hole
in his throat, hiss-clunking vent, a blurred
scan of his brain because the dark patches
made him thrash about, and so the sedation,
coma, and the Scottish consultant who said
Another infection could carry him away.

He asked if I could see plane wreckage
through the window, if he'd killed Mum
in a car crash – forgot he'd seen her earlier.
He spent an afternoon organising a conference
from his private room with ensuite, worried
there wouldn't be enough wine for the dinner.

Now he speaks to me with old-style respect.
He's polite but I miss his teasing – he should
pat my bottom or tickle me out of a hug.
I fasten his coat, I take him to the toilet.
I wish away the time till his supper is served
so I can leave without a leave-taking.

Slow Orphaning

Images slide across my lock screen at random:
hot pink rhododendrons at Kew last May,
glasses of rum and ginger on a hotel balcony.
Here's Mum, pensive and beautiful as she
gazes at the skyline from a Thames boat
when she came to see me. The last time
I tried to visit her, she said she was busy.

Dad teeing up on the ninth at Dunham
in an orange cagoule. Rain never held him back.
A heart attack slowed him. A bypass stopped him
at a stroke. His body survived fifteen years
while his mind died and I grieved for
so long. So long I was surprised
there were still tears for his funeral.

Vade Mecum

(You Post the Doris Lessing Book to me)

I love you when you reply to my email with urgency — you write in the exact way I remembered you speak — I picture your fingers moving quickly over the keyboard — wish they were finding my clitoris instead — that time your hand was under my skirt at the end of term in '96 — you left too quickly — I used to watch you dance to Cerys Matthews — planning what I would say — each time rehearsing my soliloquy — each time spoken in silence — each time hot faced with concentration — just saying goodbye in my head

Afterwards I read the book you send to me — in a film we'd know it wasn't the Doris Lessing novel with your writing inside that made the scene — it is the unwritten stage directions — the unseen asides — the way you say oral — me fantasising — you licking me out in the middle of the day –- the way you look at me intensely — wishing you were fucking me tenderly — you are the urgency I masturbate with over the bath — always when the sun is high — I think of the perfect shadow we would make

The Tide Comes in Flat

I turn the blue estuary ruby
as you watch me
from your writing shed

the water is peony up close
a mix of blood clots like jelly fish
and semen crests, red edged

I heat the water on impact
which sets the blood permanently
on the inside of my thighs

you wrap a wool cardigan bandage
onto the wrong part of me
with hands that don't understand

Hot Priest

Through a veil we kiss	hot priest
we're together under this same sheet	hot priest
you don't look away	hot priest
you look at me	hot priest
I'm your deity	hot priest
the sheet a voyeur	hot
I'm wearing lipstick	hot
the exact colour of my cervix	hot
the purple of your cock	hot
rises again	hot
we match internally	hot
we kiss for eternity	hot
you love me despite	hot
the sheet yellows with time	hot
the sheet wears out	hot
I taste of garlic	hot priest
you lick my clitoris	oh so hot priest
the sheet is a confined space	hot
my nipples little tent pegs	hot
under this frayed embrace we kiss	hot
desire heightens under cover	hot
a pearl effect on the sheet	hot
that stiffens	hot
you kiss me despite	hot priest
oh god this is good	*oh my god hot priest*
your eyes wrap around my waist	hot priest
you're everywhere	priest
I taste you everywhere	hot hot priest
the sheet dissipates	priest
absolved	love does this

Trick to Get Out of the Wedding

You have to unfold the placename before you until its crease
slips the invitation back into the envelope, which will lift
the pen from paper and remove your name from their list.
Once this is done, raise the glass back to your mouth
and quietly let the claret slip from between your lips
into the cup, so the two of you don't argue on that evening.
Now hold your right palm over the tealight on the table
and once the black cracks and hisses, reason that
this is a hand you could not use to tilt her face to yours.
After this, walk carefully to the toilets past the dancefloor
and close the door behind you, which will shut the door
that he was going to fix that night the two of you gave him dinner.
Once inside the cubicle, recite the name on the toilet before you
that will take back all the words that you learnt at school
through the discomfort of its sound - remake girls unfamiliar.
When you get back to the table, try to ignore the speeches,
because as a kid you hated public places
and everyone is worried because the child is acting oddly.
To finish, leave before the dancing, and don't answer
when they ask whether you introduced them.
Step back into the warm dark. Split apart again.

The Mark

For years I'd mistaken her narcissism for a sure sign of the easily led.
It took separation to realise that to hate yourself to that certain degree,
while convinced that your own company is the best around,
brings home the horror of the marooned. Not even mirrors to torture you,
you are your own reproduction: the perfect copy that your mind
decided long ago to set you looking at alone.
This isn't to say that, years later, when meeting, I wasn't still set on proving
that before and after all else she must be an easy mark to the vengeful.
Carrying my tools in the same hands as alcohol – I am sometimes reluctant
to tell one from the other – I'm not a particularly subtle trickster,
and most who've spent any time with me know this.
They also know that my interest alters if I catch a speck of the unexpected
in someone I'd only thought to trick. I'd let someone with cash by the bundle
falling out of their bag get away, even shield them from the plays of others,
if they mentioned something new on Anne Sexton,
or could convince me as to why the Ninth is really the best of Beethoven.
That afternoon, mind, I'd other designs, and had really worked them out,
but after a few and some more cigarettes, I saw that I'd be moving on.
Not that I'd managed to get a sentence in: she talked for two hours,
casting a galactic orbit of interlinked detail to all that passed
around her as fixed, and laying out why this system was the only one worth mentioning.
I'd thought that that would be enough to spur me on, to trick her out of something
and walk away with enough in my hand that she'd not feel the lack of til later.
But I caught myself on her second circuit. I mean, *living* like that? Wheeled in on yourself
as the orbit rots and diminishes over the years, until the final plunge of the axis?
Hadn't she already taken enough?

Blood

Listening to Scandinavian folk music played on the same instruments
that they'd have been a millennium back, I catch myself trying to hear
whether a drumskin splashed in the blood of the player
sounds different to one that isn't. I must stop reading interviews with musicians,
as this is not the first time this kind of sneakthievery's occurred
and I've tried to slip my hand under a sound, lift it softly and find something more.
Much of this has got to be down to my father, as not only do I share his blood
but his calling and pay have been dependent on
effective transubstantiation – so far as such a thing exists –
for longer than I've been alive. That being said, all I've got on dad is from
the once that I summoned the calm to ask him if he believed in all of that holy-end shit,
about it literally becoming blood, and all he gave was
'What I would say is that after you've spoken the words,
the thing being offered is not what it was.'
In the arena of the unhelpfully wise, or at least those so by intention,
my father has long reigned supreme, and this answer that – as I recall –
I took so poorly it broke my calm as a drop will a bowl,
sums up their inclination well: to offer something to transform you into blind rage;
but the something, later, is not what it was, and somehow you have more.
The substance of value, as it is on the altar, is to do with what you find you've received.
Remember that Balder, god of beauty, was brought after all from a bowl of spit,
but I doubt people brought it up either with him and that damn face,
or when taking in for the first time that most beautiful person who's just walked in.
Mind, the given and taken sometimes spend themselves in the exchange.
I remember the spatter of nosebleed dripped onto her bare chest
as we turned together after two days spent on nothing but cheap white,
rollies, and lemon-cut coke: the engine room of the poetry world.
It was different from the careful, brush-like, smearing and striping
of my chest with your blood as I held one of your hands,
and you held the rest of me. For all that we gave and took from each other,
you're still left wanting more; as I am now, leaning my ear, trying to pick out
the sound of dried blood.

TempleOS

"What people are going to read is, 'It's about a pathetic schizophrenic who made a crappy operating system.' My perspective is, 'God said I made His temple'."
— Terry A. Davis, email sent to *VICE Motherboard*, 2014

Voices may include:
Prophets, 4chan, angels,
comment threads, the Wikipedia,
the future.

All I do is go to dentists and doctors.

The hypoxia of brain cells
and physical optical media.
Be grateful for something
to lose.

All my parents do is go to dentists and doctors.

Roll your own crypto.
Cover your webcam.
Maybe God is just warm air
rising from a heatsink.

I made God's Temple, and now I am waiting for something to happen.

All you need is zero-ring total control.
Reach past the kernel, extend
yourself through silicon, and
ride a gold-lined internal BUS.

Forgive me, I forgot to remember why I love you.

First date with the Algorithm

When the Algorithm leans across to read the the cocktail menu and its arm brushes past my skin I feel a spike of haptics, and when it orders us two old fashioneds I explain I have seen *Mad Men* one and a half times but stopped halfway through the second go round because Joan Harris' relationship breakdown was too closely mirroring my own situation, and the Algorithm smiles patiently and asks if this is a story I often tell on first dates, and I say yes because it is relatable and opens up further meaningful conversation, and I feel that the Algorithm gets it and I find this refreshing, so I ask the Algorithm what it is like to be burdened by prescience, and the Algorithm tells me it is very good at catching lobsters but cannot break their shells or eat them, and I look into the sands of its silicon eyes and I see traffic and the weather and geopolitics, and I imagine us together, our handsome yacht anchored to the swirling outer rim of the Great Pacific Garbage Patch, as we watch the consumer grade electricals float by. The Algorithm asks how my lockdown went and I list all the bad things that happened but then I say that on reflection I learnt a lot about myself and it replies yes me too.

Jay Leno's Apple Watch

There's something in the air tonight.
Bouncing the California skyline,
it spots me, careens down toward the Strip,
a hot clutch of encrypted message
landing on my arm like an insect.
I feel its sharp actuation —
a friend from the club days;
a summons for coffee
with the sundrenched King
of Neilson households, King
of late night, King Shit, yes
King.

June

The Tomb of Edgar Allan Poe

after Mallarmé

Eternity has wrought the final change
– he has become himself, still holding his blade
against the age's throat. He will not fade;
he saw Death's victory, made it newly strange.

As when the angel came; the mob once heard
him purify their worn-down tribal words.
Drunk, their tongues all thick, they gibbered, slurred;
cast out his spells, the truths they found absurd.

Out of hostile soil and cloud, comes grief
from which to try to sculpt a bas-relief
to ornament the dazzling tomb of Poe.

This calm block, fallen from unknown disaster,
may mark the bounds, where none beyond dare go
to the black flights of Blasphemy, the forever after.

Toad

after "Le Crapaud" by Tristan Corbière (1845-75)

Listen! There's a song this airless night.
See that slice of shiny tin? Moonlight,
a cut-out backdrop of deep green dark.

A song: its vibrely creaky echo
from the rockery beyond the decking.
It's shut its gob. Let's have a dekko!

Toad! Why are you so scared of me?
I'm your faithful servant. Don't you know it?
Just look at him: a baldy, wingless poet.
Junk-dump nightingale. Singing... horribly.

Well, is it really such an awful croak?
Can't you see the bright glint in his eye?
No? He's buggered off, crawled beneath his rock.
Old toady-boyo's really me – Okey-Doke.

Goodbye!

Lullabye-bye

a sort of Rondel for After, after Tristan Corbière; from "Rondels pour après"

It's getting dark, child, stealer of sparks.
There are no more nights. There are no more days.
Sleep... waiting for those girls who'd remark
now how they'd "Never!", then how they'd "Always!"

Do you hear their steps? So light on their little feet.
How love has wings, flies and sings like the lark.
It's getting dark, child, stealer of sparks.

Do you hear their voices? The cellar's deaf and black.
Sleep as light as the trees snug in their bark.
Your friends, the bears, they won't be coming back
or hurling rocks at the ladies in the park.
It's getting dark, child, stealer of sparks.

charlie wave

ANTI the letters that comprise the opening line
ANTI patterns of silk on a handful of silk
ANTI light of tangerine sunset on tangerine pool
ANTI the fourth line being absent of hook
ANTI fresh fruit fed to rotten children
ANTI philosophers at the window
ANTI hi...
ANTI plastic sun   ANTI   virgin moon
ANTI your grandmother shopping for a suit in tesco
ANTI spasmodic basement dancers electrifying a fawn
ANTI vegetating mid-career poets peeing onto mirrors
ANTI orange salad served by romans in space glasses
ANTI self immolation by nuns
   fight them with your claws   sisters !
ANTI adam the egg & eve the egg layer
ANTI vladimir putin stroking pandas in the satanic zoo
ANTI lesbian exploitation of lesbians drowning in laudanum
ANTI binary love song eating non binary code
ANTI that you have stopped reading
ANTI 'charlie wave' sung by rihanna   madonna   hannah arendt
ANTI *any* person of voice & style more beautiful than charlie
ANTI swirl of neon in black hole caffeine glitch   ANTI nothing
ANTI ow!
ANTI brunch with juliet binoche without a top hat
ANTI you   ANTI your nightmares   ANTI your awful frock
ANTI your god-awful taste
ANTI the tears glittering in your beard
ANTI everything that has come
ANTI everything that will follow
ANTI everything that shares the truth of ANTI
ANTI charlie wave   but not
ANTI the dolphins riding the happy seas
ANTI letters that do not comprise the final line

PRO charlie

pink champagne at the pony club

the second step was a rose blossoming
under impure light, paper tablecloth,
image of drowned bee; a galaxy born

in the hollow of a spoon, the nun i loved
loved a number of nuns. told me,
the bible was a prose poem for the moon.

i wept ribbons onto her jaguar.
on the racecourse i drank
pink champagne at the pony club,

jesuits ripped the radio up, a girl
gave me a daisy chain that went on forever,

balled over to me in leather boots,
put my foot through the table, since then
i've been trying to stay in the now.

night moves

small pieces of wing washed up along the shore
branches of sleep strung with starflowers
satchels of dreams protected by thieves
if you know who you are
know who you are
who you are

the long candle casts pools of light over the bedroom floor
oceanic light where ships are sinking
night is so heavy
it will take cranes to lift her
beyond the door

new worlds are opening in the hum of distant spheres
the owls carry petty crimes in their feathers, pray
what good would it do?
why are you running away?
why are you running away from me?

Gull Season

Gulls love summer
take flight south
as soon as the schools are out.

Huers no longer call from cliffs,
gulls take their place
watching town not wave,

cawing hevva
when they see a free perch
on low tide harbour.

One sits on a bench
chip in beak,
ketchup drip on lower bill,

complaining about flocks
filling their space
they say:

'How lovely is the beach,
how quaint the cobbled streets
and friendly fisher cottages.'

When winter's chill
calls them home to roost
a local, one of the few

who stays when the gulls come,
taps a sign nearby.
'Don't feed the gulls' it says.

But we do.
They come every year
whether we feed them or not.

An Edhen Varow

My a wrug diskudha an edhen varow
a-bervedh y'n liverva goth.
Y fluvennow o papier maché bleudh
ow trehedhes a-dreus y eskern hedor
kepar ha gwelynni yn-dann troos.

My a vynn bos mar glys avel a'n edhen na –
yn kosk distrogh gans an jydh splann,
yn kres distrogh pan usi'n bys
ow tiskwedhes y enep gwir,
pluvogow a-dro dhe'm skovornow.

My a omwovyn,
eus bywnans gans y deylu?
My a omwovyn a's byrlansow a yeunons i?
glas hag byw kepar ha'y fluvennow tawesek –
kepar ha tas anteythi kewsel a gerensa,
gans chons vyth namoy y leverel.

The Dead Bird

I uncovered the dead bird
within the old library.
His feathers were papier maché soft
reaching across his bones, fragile
as bedding under foot.

I want to be as cosy as that bird –
in sleep unbroken by the bright day,
in peace unbroken by the world
revealing its true face,
pillows around my ears.

I wonder,
are his family alive?
I wonder if they miss his hugs –
blue and alive like his silent feathers,
like a father unable to speak of love
with no more chance to say it.

Hippopotamouse

she is not a fool
if and only if a thief
a gray sieve driven
the river horse is sinking

riven habitat
exit in boiling water

hippopotamus
I will so hold your horses
herd to dale to bloat
little humpbacked horse ballet
it is informal
if fossil whales school themselves

Hag Gift

related to witch
cut and dried for use as fuel
peat to jet lignite
if habit through habitat
angel and monster
accumulate sphagnum moss
so we are ugly
bryophytes from oyster green

so we are ugly
bogs of mostly soft water
peat to jet lignite
cut and dried for use as fuel
angel and monster
bryophytes from oyster green

The Macbeth Protocol

Erinaceinae
thrice and once the urchin-pig
whined not mine, not mine
the scent past tense the first witch
needs under the hedge
sleeping through and through thunder

the familiar
hedge-pig will poison her own
keratin needles
she will anoint the unknown
once and future scent
the froth comes from her mouth from

the experiment
in the cauldron pure and cold
in all alcohol
floats and floats and floats and floats
one ingredient
dissolves and dissolving clean

is the land urchin
to hibernate through and through
her discovery
saves her witch, her coven, and
yields paclitaxel
bark of yew tree chewed and chewed

my body, brown

a playground
for melanin politics

battered in beds
where often sex
is a patriarchal discourse
a geopolitical nuisance.

(and, they all want me to love my body)

but i have grown sick
                        of   loving
                                             bodies,
cities   made   of   bodies,
sickness made   of   bodies,
love   made   of   bodies;
                        love, doesn't make the body.

on nights when baba makes obscure bangla literary references
to সুহাসিনীর পমেটম by কমলকুমার মজুমদার a novel without
punctuation maa fears that i have started to mourn in devanagari
memory is substratal and maa does not know how to console
my polyglot grief i wonder if bangla without the oxford comma
is what my inner monologue should be i have hence found all
synonyms for abandonment and reduced them to a ten-milligram
dosage of escitalopram my sad white deus ex machina wrapped in
foil the only habit i remember not to break

within the body

grief is without

punctuation

never

pausing

a seance for my friend.

dead at twenty-five.

too much meth in his veins, not enough jaggery.

a december baby.

upon birth, he was fed sugar stirred coconut.

every birthday, hence, he awaited my return from darjeeling.

"mimi, first. then, cake."

and i was only seventeen, when he said he loved me.

and i need to believe he is dead, maa.

he won't ever look at me, hidden behind memories.

are these my roots, maa- cirrhosis, drug abuse, fiscal debt, abortions?

July

anton yelchin

i am thinking of a dent in a set of iron railings;
how the bend backwards still aches in the struts
as if, even now, these bars are straining
to pull away from their wrought framework,

the spine's final, awful contortion.
they're reporting that he was an actor, a young man
with kiss-curl hair and dimpled cheeks, still keen
to talk about stanislavski. they're printing his face
in an oval beside a photograph of the damaged fence,
and i am thinking of him pinned there like a butterfly,
his lungs fluttering in the darkness. they're saying it
probably took a full minute and asking what he was
thinking stood there with the engine running.
perfect posture. isadora duncan. nobody's watching.

freak accident, they're calling it,
and i am thinking of how some things
can creep up on you, like a jeep rolling
backwards down the drive,
whilst you're facing the other way.

cosmonaut

from the front step,
    my grandfather watches the sky
        for something going up,

    while the old dog next-door remembers
        his howl,

thinks of gagarin
        lighting the vast darkness,
    a struck match,

    the cruelness of making him go alone,

squints at the stars, waits

        until the dog quiets.

whatever he's looking for
just keeps getting further away.

    he sighs,
        turns once more
    to the empty rooms
        of his house.

werewulf

how many nights
      beneath god's milk-white left eye

     to become
        to howl?

we stuck things are
      creatures
        not seen as we should be,

  fixed under your gaze.

mother, bring me my funeral suit
        my black winter coat.

    let's bury my womb
      grant it rest
        in this piece of earth.

call me by my blue name.
  slip *jonathan* from your lips
     as if it means *love*

       — because mama it does.

Who's that
            whistle in the distant
kitchen
                        kettle going
spray arc
            panorama whiplash
froth down scroll
                        white sea-script
pulse of old
                        buy habits
tea pools on the
                        sunburst
day supplied
                        resolve to
more past tense
                        in silence
thoughts so
            wingful black scatter
in the green
            bleached clumps
and wet teeth rattle
                        at the skylights

Noup Head
          catching the sun
far off this cloud
          one toothpick
its dear
          regular light
when dark
          goes over
my maudlin boat
          pitched in TV
yawing
          Belgravia
of Waterloo
          bright picture
bubo yawns but
          get this
cat mouths
          Julian Fellowes
will see you now
     the reef screams wave
streams foam
     and our own day

now plumes off
             still was
the mummy assembly
             heads I know
unreachable
             the wind in ruins
lives together
             when *I* see you again
I will hold you and
             hold you
then whistle
    come back to your senses
and the kettle and
             rounding the corner
into the kitchen
                    Brian
legs noodled
             in the green chair
and says
    welcome to the history
of Great Britain
                    numbnuts

A POEM, SLANT

A Statement of Poetics for 'Lunette'

de Chirico's *The Double Dream of Spring*

A poem is a mouth discussing itself. A poem is a half-thought thing. A poem flirts with its stanzas. A poem frames itself kaleidoscopically. A poem is concrete.

Newman's *Canto VII*

A poem is a box of words. A poem is ground down. A poem is mechanical so grease it up, pull its lever, and watch it spin. A poem displays two shades of the same colour. A poem is water, is water, is water.

Deren and Hammid's *Meshes of the Afternoon*

A poem's face, a mirror. A poem looks into itself. A poem repeats itself. A poem repeats. A poem is monochromatically technicolour. A poem waits.

Buñuel and Dalí's *An Andalisian Dog*

A poem is a moon. A poem is the furthermost point from the reader. A poem cuts open the eye and the eye cuts open the poem. A poem is the gut reaction. A poem sticks, gargoyled.

Kandinsky's *Lyrical*

A poem is automatism. A poem keeps us afloat. A poem is a bird, is an ear, is a spine, is a bird. A poem is a science we read with closed eyes.

Martin's *Tremolo*

A poem is the Anglican Cathedral. A poem is obsession. A poem is the underwater effect. A poem is a flang. A poem is your father at one pillar and you at the other, listening to his words as they travel through arched sandstone: *there are times with him times when he holds my hand and rubs with his thumb times when we dance times when we laugh, we laugh, we laugh.*

Onwuemezi's *Dark Neighbourhood*

A poem opens itself up. A poem is dissection. A poem is the layerings of dreamscapes and landscapes. A poem is a block of prose, exposed, breathing, alive. A poem is the dialogues we have.

Magritte's *The Double Secret*

A poem is a thought mask. A poem is underbellied. A poem is cogged. A poem empathises. A poem is the factory. A poem is the image, the repression, the relief.

Egger's *The Lighthouse*

A poem is a lonely thing. A poem is shot in square 1.19:1 aspect ratio. A poem uses light, bends light, keeps light, tight tight tight. A poem is the audience still watching.

Hockney's *Six Fairy Tales*

A poem is cross hatched. A poem is a thinking thing and it thinks of its posture on the page. A poem will chop itself up and slot itself into the reader's mouth like a diced carrot. A poem is you sitting on the gallery bench behind me. A poem is your kiss.

Iványi's *Wind*

A poem is a one-shot short film. A poem is panoramic. A poem reveals itself when its ready.

Weerasethakul's *Blue*

A poem is the bonfires reflection. A poem sleeps. A poem is the props and parts of a stage. A poem is a falling theatre. A poem reveals itself as two alternate landscapes.

Carax's *Holy Motor's*

A poem doesn't make sense. A poem doesn't have to. A poem watches your expression and Leos chuckles. A poem is a garage of talking limousines. A poem wears a motion capture suit one moment. A poem dances with chimpanzees the next.

Lowry's *Man Lying on a Wall*

A poem waits.

Gluck's *Landscape with a Church Tower*

A poem is a small strip of land below the absolute. A poem is a bowl, not a flat backcloth. A poem is two-dimensionally three-dimensional.

Twombly's *Cold Stream*

A poem is automatism before the solid word. A poem breathes. A poem is a coryphée with a stick of chalk. A poem repeats itself. A poem is immortal. A poem is beyond us but we exhibit claustrophobia.

Arp's *What Violins Sing in their Bed of Lard*

A poem translates through defamiliarisation. A poem is the crust she doesn't want. A poem is the crust you eat.

Fellini's *8½*

A poem doesn't need subtitles. A poem is a line of passengers stood up in a coach decapitated by the frame of the window.

De Chirico's *Geometry of Shadows*

A poem has cousins and its cousins hang in galleries. A poem negotiates the parts of the canvas unstretched. A poem sits in the hammocked space between weaves.

Escher's *Puddle*

A poem is an eye. A poem looks through you, darkly.

Gormley's *Matrix* series

A poem is an overlapping thing. A poem is a magician. A poem makes it look easy. A poem is the simplest version of itself.

Hopper's *Chair Car*

A poem borrows colours from a Giorgio sky. A poem elongates itself into a one-point perspective. A poem sits, waits, and travels sideways on a moving locomotive. A poem always wears its shadows.

Friedrich's *The Abbey in the Oakwood*

A poem is barbed and electrocuted and twigged. A poem is ruins. A poem is a silhouette of its former, current, and future self.

Millet's *The Angelus* & Dalí's *Archaeological Reminiscence of Millet's Angelus*

A poem exists for a later poem to reflect. A poem is the dialogues we have with our visitors. A poem is the dialogues we have after sex, during grief, and on Thursday evenings.

Hoffman's *Music Out Of The Moon: Music Unusual Featuring The Theremin*

A poem is the signal from another species. A poem is the first thought of a canal system. A poem is flat until a swam lands. A poem names itself Lunette and the poet nods, smiles, writes.

Bowie's *Blackstar*

Wearing an old suit, aged like a musician, talking with its former self, bedridden and anticipatory, a poem is always an epilogue.

Convalescence

Se hisser hors de la chambre sépulcrale
Et du cercueil du cerveau. Apercevoir
Les branches du cerisier : grands cygnes en vol
Aux ailes rayonnantes de fleurs.
Se courber au-dessus de la chrysalide
Des non-nés et du cantique de leurs crânes.

« Qu'as-tu fait, crient-ils, qu'as-tu fait
De ta chevelure de lilas blancs et de ta robe
Transparente en rumeurs de fleurs de cerisier ?

-L'alchimiste caboche les a calcinées.
La fournaise de la mémoire les a noircies.
Je neige de pétales foudroyés.
La neige est bègue. La bouche bâillonnée
Haillonnée de mots sans repos. »

Convalescence

Hoist oneself out of the sepulchral bedroom
And the coffin of the brain. Observe
The branches of the cherry tree: great swans in flight,
Their wings radiant with blossoms.
Bend over the chrysalis
Of the unborn and the canticle of their skulls.

"What have you done, they cry, what have you done
To your white-lilac hair and your dress
Transparent in rumours of cherry trees?

— The alchemical bonce has burnt them to a cinder.
The furnace of memory has blackened them.
I snow blasted petals.
The snow is stuttering. The gagged mouth
Is tattered with restless words".

Bégaiement

Cratère de fatigue, ventrale, cervicale. Assez.
La lumière d'hiver crie d'anges que je ne peux rejoindre.
La douleur tord la chevelure d'hortensia de la mémoire.
Une voix de ruminant bégaie à l'oreille :
« Dieu me meut ». Ou est-ce : « Dieu me
Ment » ? Le destin se joue à la lettre près
Et on n'entend pas distinctement cette lettre.
Mais le tapage cesse. Un peu de bleu monte au crâne.
Chaque côte est peinte en or par un peintre invisible :
Échelle intérieure à gravir jusqu'à l'œil du cœur.

Stuttering

Crater of fatigue. Ventral. Cervical. Enough.
The light of winter cries angels I cannot join.
Grief twists the hortensia hair of memory.
A ruminant's voice stutters in the ear:
God moves me. Or does God lie to me?
Destiny is played out to the letter.
One does not hear this letter clearly.
But the uproar ceases. A touch of blue rises in the skull.
Each rib is painted in gold by an invisible painter:
Interior ladder to climb up to the heart's core.

Ghost-Walking
Dunoon Pier 26th June 1957

Ten years since last sight of you   you reappear

four feet in front of me   dawdling down the pier

     with an aspiring Hepburn and Loren

slingbacks snagging on the slats   wide polka dot skirts

sunglasses slipping   down your upturned noses

     three feet   past an anoraked grandfather

pipe trailing smoke like a steam train's chimney

     stroll a pair of celluloid starlets   and you

Dunoon's Glasgow-accented answer to Dorothy Dandridge

     cradling newsprint chips in the crook of your arm

licking your fingers after each bite   salt speckling

     the scarlet-slicked sheen of your lips

         two feet   your laugh carries

there's a canted tilt to your chin   I never could fit

     to any family member living   one

     you've chemically straightened and set your hair

I miss the natural curve   the strength I had to learn

     to twist and tame it   into cornrows   or bantu knots

But your skin is the same   still two shades darker

     than milk splashed tea   you brush past

     apologise   glance back

     over your shoulder as you recede out of shot

your father's eyes appear darker   set in my face

     they remain blank   unknowing   I hang back

scuttle forward   dodging contortionists   unicyclists

     toffee apple hawkers   watch you weaving away

through the crowd   laughing   the turbulent wake

of other holidaymakers   conceals a tiny   headscarfed

woman with ease   you leave the crowd   but

     I am bound to the boards

training the pier's telescope   on your silhouettes
        a string of paper dolls linked at the arms
I lose my shillings   willingly   one by one
as I chase your matchstick figure's stretching shadow
        juddering along the strandline
as if from   cell to cell   of unspooling film
        until the coins run out   you disappear
with the clacking wind-down of celluloid on capstan
I descend to the sand   linger in the lee of the pier's posts
neck craning for a better view   digging my fingers
into my bag's handle to quell the stretching itch in my palms
        I wait   watch you recede into the dark
follow remnants of the path you left   through settling grains
        seeking your footprints in falling light   stepping
where you stepped   until all fades to black.

30th March 1851 — 3 Bowling Green Yard, Sheffield

Column added for town and county of birth

Sit, tap the nib on the inkwell's rim, there's little left to fill in.

Beside the children, the husband you acquired seven years

before the first finally died, your line lies blank, waiting.

Time to reclaim what you once shed walking — limping —

down that westward driven crack of a road heading towards

Yorkshire's snaggle-toothed border. The grass stretching out

on all sides. Flat, like a pane of bottle-green glass, marred

only by a bubble six inches off the horizon. A stand of trees,

the desiccated bones of a farmhouse perhaps. Time short,

you did not stop to wonder. Limbs aching, stumbled, tripped,

a bit of yourself slipped from your palms into the rut of a cart

track and you did not miss it for miles. For the first time since

you turned your back to the Stump's long shadow, you feel it,

a wave beaching far inland. Home landing in your lap once more.

Sarah Hardman. Married. Age thirty-four. Place of Birth: Boston.

31st March 1901 — 14 Tide Waiter's Row, Kirkdale, Liverpool

6 years before The Deceased Wife's Sister's Marriage Act

I am born a dead docker's daughter,
raised in Toxteth Park, Lancashire,
in the lee of the Herculaneum Basin,
thirty years after the Pottery cracked,
petroleum slick in the roots of my hair,
sandstone under the beds of my nails.

I am your wife's widowed sister,
who lost a man to wind and waves
thirty days after I married him,
beached up on your front step
with no children, no pension,
just the clothes I stood in, a smile.

I am your first-floor parlour lodger,
no need for cook or scullery maid,
my sister sacks them all. I will serve.
I sleep by the hearth with the dog
and, on nights when thunder cracks
the casement, your youngest daughter.

I am your fourth child's birth mother.
There is no word for me. No category
to fit me in — ribs, knees, elbows
and all. Compressed down to syllables,
I do not make sense. A lie will have to do.
Anna Louise Ellison. Boarder. Thirty-two.

9

When this fisheye planetarium, which drains the unilateral dark,
            demotes each motored zone to an involuntary park
re-enclosed beneath the sign of its biomorphic trademark,

         with their risk-averse protections indefectibly severe,
wireless tremors shuttle down the untapped asthenosphere
     where relics of the sunken day—deposited from anywhere—

unpick their abandoned particles. Astray in a metagalaxy,
       such multiplex arrangements stay stochastically unfree
to flare up like a flock within a katabatic wind; by proxy

        emergent properties of ant mills growing infinite
leak through multiplayer persistent state worlds to evaporate
     in holographic cloud forests, hollowed out by searchlight.

On the flipside of this flight simulation—through these readymade
        smart glasses buffered by the sun's invasive aubade—
pandistributed glidepads tip their scales and cells to intergrade

        intrinsic chronotypes with each peripheral device
in need of an adaptor for modems to decentralize
     filamentous texture maps stamped with microgravities.

14

As some chance-based sibylline actuary
        puts decision trees in place to maim
    polymorphic underpinnings—altered by the same
           crescive impulse, aimed with the inevitability
  of multiclass perceptrons thrown forward to reclaim
          bioinformation   out   of   cytotoxicity
        fraught with self-enveloping autolysis—
denaturants backpropagate themselves into the blue
    more omissive than a desubmerged oasis
for each tegument to viralize its blotted residue
    decorrelating regions of vicariance, off cue
              with the other's coexistences in tow;
     yet for heatstruck glaciations, liquid state machines somehow
        regenerate from their global distillation's afterglow
  presequenced by a sensorineural megawatt
drawing rein from stormclouds—buffered off and on
          by a polar expiration's macrocyclic antiphon,
   hypercatalectically outdistancing the overwrought
        intermodulations hammered down each micron-
     scaled conduit, bound towards a cognizant expansion slot—
      whose turbulences, thickening in catalytic rings,
          open out through portal sites to nowhere
   where helitacks make heatwaves' thermal profilings
     doomscroll down the anticommons' tragic disrepair
gamethrown by regime shifts inoperable as vapourware, ˙
      while the scope creep of duplexed interoperability
  lets slide the season creep and sub-replacement fertility
  of conurbations zoned off by a fintech-domed city.

18

Go, then pause each dream's subpar
           precircumstance whose costs outshoot
your free hand with a steel polestar,
         gearing up to plug the route
where single-use white goods impounding
      breathing rooms in taskbars pending
         type
            what hype
floats the dross on every holotype.

In profile, all your backlogged habits
          track you down, then scrape the basis
underneath which spring submits
        skewed kernels to kurtosis;
still none of this, when validating
         asset models recreating
          solid air
            from software,
can tell where your eigenfaces are.

While their hidden lives survive your own
          through interfaces making dents
in caches amortized on loan
        from ransomware investments,
every public chain that fails to stop
         has factored in your drag and drop
         indifference
          to permanence,
refreshed in mined translucence.

August

Another Swan

I'm right
on the steps of a
hall. Hubris.
It helped the
heaving of having
been there in some
same past. That is all
where I lived, for
my changes. Sky
neutral and bone-
ready. I was ready. A boy
bluffed he wasn't.
I couldn't change
pronounishly. Oh
I hummed him but
can I be fluent
about myself. About
the plus or minus
light of day I do this in.
And am there for.

Virgil

Just like a snake a bronze wheel crushes on the road
an offshoot or overgrowth of them, I see
    or one smashed by a traveler's cruel stone:
that bush, so the overgrowth becomes a home that any
    mangled and half-dead, it's desperate
one with wings can use, claim, customize, occupy, add
    to, glad, glide away but can't. It keeps coiling
bits to make it on your own. Not sure why
    its long body, fiercely rearing up, its neck
the goal. Even a haircut has to converge
    hissing, eyes like fire; but the maimed part drags
with something else we've seen before,
    down, and the snake weaves knots and falls back,
so loneliness doesn't seem to apply. The lone
    on itself: so the ship limped under oars.
Twig doesn't raise an eyebrow. My eyebrow
    still, it spread full sails and reached the port.

The Second He

"Don't be so careful," Dan said to me, the second he
slammed the blue hatchback's back down.
The speed he picked up, from there to here, became a demo.
I liked to play the footage back:
I was withstanding (I was grieving
the disappearing he was doing) that life, because of how
we were together. The same shut-eyed look
his face became when he walked away, in sun-
light, following a line.

"Maybe all I have to be's myself more strange and
true," I said, in a mirror
manner. It was early spring. The magenta snow shovel leaned against
the white railing. A yellow one, better, sturdier,
with range, also. It was like early spring. "Same
thing." Like a bad faith actor at the end of his line. "Maybe
maybe not." The slow local flora and
fauna didn't belong then. I opened my eyes.
Pieces of the words disappearing all the
time. The show of shoes. "Careful." Car-ful.

לֹא הוּרַק

לֹא הוּרַק, לֹא יוּרַק
כִּיס הַכְּאֵב הַכָּחֹל,
מַטְבְּעוֹת קָשׁוֹת
אֲצוּרוֹת לָכֶם
לְשָׁי רוּחִי לַתֹּהַג.

אֵיךְ הִשְׁפַּלְתֶּם שָׁמַי
עַד כִּי הֵרַמְתִּי יָדַי לְשֵׂאתָם,
אֵיךְ סְכַכְתֶּם עֵינַי מִן הָאוֹר
עַד כִּי הָלַכְתִּי לְבַקֵּשׁ מְנוֹרוֹת,
אֵיךְ רְמַסְתֶּם אֶת שְׁתִילֵי הַחוֹלְמִים
עַד כִּסִּיתִים גַּם מִגְּשֶׁם וְשָׁמֶשׁ.

לֹא עוֹד הִתְעַנַּגְתִּי עַל פְּרִיחַת הָאָדָם
כְּיֶלֶד בַּבֹּקֶר-בַּבֹּקֶר.
סוֹמֵר לָעַד בְּשַׂר לִבִּי
אֶת זִכְרוֹן פְּנֵיכֶם הַחֵרְשִׁים אֶל הַצְּלִיל
הַנּוֹקֵב, הַחוֹתֵךְ, הַקּוֹרֵעַ.

נִבְהָל וְנוֹדֵד,
נוֹטֵר אֹהָלִים וְשַׁלֶּכֶת,
גַּם כִּי אֵשֵׁב בְּבֵית אֵל חֹם סִיר וָדֶלֶת
יִפְּלוּ עָלַי כְּתָלָיו בְּעוֹדָם נִצָּבִים,
יִכְבַּד מַנְעוּלוֹ בִּגְרוֹנִי.

מְסַדְּרֵיכֶם הֶגַחְתִּי עוֹטֶה סַדִּיכֶם
נָקְשֶׁה אֵיבָרִים בִּכְפוֹר פַּחַד-זַעַם
בְּאֵינְסְפוֹר אַשְׁמוּרוֹת יָרֵא וְכָמַהּ
מַמְתִּין וְדָרוּךְ עַל עוֹלָמִי הַנּוֹתָר.

(מִתּוֹךְ "כִּיס הַכְּאֵב הַכָּחֹל" 1980)

Not Emptied

The blue pocket of pain
hasn't been emptied, will not be emptied,
of hard coins
treasured for you,
who kneaded my spirit into formlessness.

How you lowered my sky
till I raised my hands to carry it,
how you screened my eyes from light
till I went in search of lamps,
how you trampled the seedlings of my dreams
till I covered them even from sun and rain.

No longer did I take pleasure in the flowering of man
like a child in the dawn of day.
Forever the flesh of my heart is riven
by the memory of your faces, deaf
to the piercing, tearing sound.

Frightened, wandering,
guarding my tent and fallen leaves
even if I sit at home, by the warmth of pots and doors,
its walls implode on me where they stand,
and its lock is heavy in my throat.

I emerged from your pillories wearing them,
my limbs frost-stiffened by anger and fear,
full of dread and desire every hour all night,
guarding the remains of my world.

(1980)

וְאִם אֶפְתַּח

וְאִם אֶפְתַּח אֶת לִבִּי
הַאִם תָּעוּף הַצִּפּוֹר לַחָפְשִׁי?
אֵין לָדַעַת מִי כָּלוּא שָׁם –
אוּלַי זֶה חָתוּל מְעוֹפֵף,
אוּלַי צִפּוֹר בְּמַגָּפַיִם.

יוֹם אַחַר יוֹם, שָׁנָה אַחַר שָׁנָה
הוֹלֶכֶת וְשָׁבָה חַיַּת הָעֶצֶב
מְסוֹרָג אֶל סוֹרָג,
מְצִיצָה מִן הֶחָזֶה
בַּאֲנָשִׁים הַחוֹלְפִים עַל פָּנֶיהָ.

אֵין לָדַעַת מִי אֲנִי.
יֵשׁ לִי עֶשֶׂר אִמָּהוֹת, וְאֵין לִי אַבָּא.
לְבַסּוֹף הָפַכְתִּי לְאַרְנָב –
הוּא בּוֹרֵחַ, וַאֲנִי
מַפִּיל אוֹתוֹ בִּירִיָּה אַחַת,
מֵכִין תַּבְשִׁיל אַרְנָבִים
וְאוֹכֵל.

And If I Open

And if I open my heart
will the bird fly to freedom?
Who knows what's imprisoned in there –
maybe it's a flying puss,
maybe a bird in boots.

Day by day, year after year,
the sadness-animal paces
behind bars,
peeking out from my chest
at the passing people.

There's no telling who I am.
I have ten mothers and no father.
Finally, I turn into a rabbit –
he runs away, and I
shoot him down with a single shot,
prepare rabbit stew
and eat.

How to Pronounce Dagenham
For Jodie Chesney

First relax ur froat, ur maaf, ur vibe
Not much to do about not much to do so ya chat shit:
Wiv ya white shirt unbuttoned over West Ham strip
Clanging pawnshop platinum on a baby blackbird's chest.
Narmy Army swells over Heathway, trailing broken Dagz like
'U wot mate?' Fist tatts, clapbacks, my brother's best mate got...

that C2C tracks constant clanging
in her veins, she got a lulled goodbye to Percy, to the pawnshop
goodbye to Jo: sun glows platinum
through her, straight to the grass on
which she sits. not much to do about not much to do, a
purple bracelet twirls, lip corners curl when he calls her 'baby'
soft as sweet tarmac, watching blackbirds
crows? crows watch back. breath rises, settles, in her chest

Which flowers in Foxglove, which blossoms in Columbine:
She gavvers em. Playgrand wood chips skitter to soften the earf on which she
sits.
Not
much
to
do
about
Not
much
to
do,
a

Rupture

We lay together in liminal space, in utter disgrace
unable to leave the zone of discomfort
to contort ourselves beyond projection
Anonymous and lonely, unproductive and alive

How can you tell photoshop from fate?
When the mouth moves so convincingly

When the mouth movements are so convincingly aligned, it's deep
They make you say whatever they want.
Make you say: *More, more, more*
Make you say: *My discomfort is illusion*
and rest is for the weak.

You've been here before
so kick the brick from out your lip
Kick misguided faith in the all powerful 'L'
train to non-place, to hyperdrive
through overheated junkspace
Formless, shapeless, endless

You, half empty, again. Left between everyone and no one,
like tipped chair on stained carpet, like a window left ajar
Anonymous and lonely, unproductive and alive
Again
The imprint of your intervention lay eerie on my breast

Again
Again
Again
Again
Again

A Field Guide to Getting Lost

At horizon, inhale
Towards an open window
And if the sun calls you,
Accept.

At exit, inspect the earth
For passing insects,
Welcome them by name and
Move.

At corner, allow the breeze
To tease your unwashed hair
Use your hands to follow
Suit.

At exhale, angels whisper
Under oak. Each leaf calls you
Lost. Each leaf calls you
Home.

The Heart Pushes Out, The Heart Rests

Every bloodied nose
    assessed in relation to
anatomies of the skull. Clothes
      filled out unbeknownst to time or
the graduations of a belt notch. *Sleep*
suppressant. Vested interests in the grey
    shades of skin, blood moon held
beneath eyelid. There are two of us
      here, you have spoken to us both.
We lied, the same as the chocolate and
      damson lied to your tongue. It isn't
difficult to split into two when partitioned by
      glass. We, and by that I mean us, deny all
in the same way a river denies the weight of
      a dying salmon. To float down
    rapids as two separate pieces of a
knotted branch. *The bears are on their haunches.*
    The ovaries, full of roe, ripe for the pawing.
Laid bare on the rocks, your mouth stained with
      Auburn is fear. *This is our ceremony.*
    Pressure is an ending, a snake's tongue.
Choose between starvation or rebirth into an
      estuary mouth. Water once known as cloud,
      once seen stabbed upon the knife of a
mountaintop. Deliver me from trances, from
    tricks of the light. Scare me towards the
        fate of a dead man gasping his
          way back to life.

Second Shadow Competition

To climb up a hill so *Serpentine,* and then
  to find it. Above the sky held hostage with

wires across its neck. Simple whistle of song a
  train pulled early into dusk, and tortured by

vastness, a pastel palette. Upwards from the
  tail with heart in hand, a fear of hardening,

the firmness of a rosehip. 'Till at its peak, wind
  pacing four- legged, the tilt of a broken-

necked bird, *tumultuous.* A reddening tongue,
  a dewy red lip. Resting to feel the tightening

rope drag away summer's auburn worthlessness.
  Knowing not of love but asking to feel it.

Forgetting what it was, *the purpose,* but plentiful
  fields. Of bites abrupt, pink with lusciousness.

Mediating Extinction Level Event

Children dance around a maypole. Red ribbon to yellow,
a navy blue, the sky shrouded with all our collective relief
flown at half-mast. *It must be the end.* A herd of liquorice
horses in the liquid field. This nostalgia smells like summer
salad. The way she used to roll the ham next to the egg, some
slices of bleeding apple. I wish I could have loved myself the
way I loved you. *Abrasion remembrance list* played in-staccato.
The blood runs away from the fingers, the pick-axe says hello
to the head. Fontanelles steeled in militaristic drum stroke
rudiment pattern as fireworks jabbed into cracks of pavement
are unable to dissolve. All hollowed out and spent. So quietly
seasonless. I hear the membraned voices downstairs creeping
in the yellow light of two conversant ghosts. Silhouette of
lonely bear twisted into tailfeather of comet, worn as scarf.
How many times should I disappoint this earth. Loose smiles
for every botched expression held in hand. How could I never
hold *yours* It is ending and the sea is perfectly still. We set fire
to our clothes. All dead swans knock together like wood.

Normalise Knife Fighting Your Therapist

Today the papers, in the West at least, are heavy with corrections. The body of the unidentified man washed up in Avonmouth was in fact a wasp nest set with rhinestone & pearl typewriter keys; the Bristol cryptids found stealing canopic jars were activists grown over by forests. In the flat above a fish & chip shop, in Keynsham, the river museum archivists have discovered a new species living in the exhibits rather than the biomes they represent. They won't speak of it. You dream sour. Waking up is revisionist propaganda that *no, it's always been this way.* The wind is leading the day to the type of danger you'd need a new god to navigate, but the schools are broken for the season & the motorways are a packed congregation of family worship praying for the sea. Escape is a kind of hope. I heard from reliable sources that you have been looking into mirrors in your dreams. You're telling yourself you can get through this again. But you can't. All the people found in mirrors are staging a tournament to appoint your successor. They line up in your reflection to see which one you most believe is you &, having access to your memories, they do a pretty good impression of you but also of being OK which you have never done so if you know what to look for it's easy to figure out who's real. You've been looking to prove you are real for so long now. I hear your dreams are the type in which your home gets bigger the longer you stay there. I hear you are dreaming of burning churches for getting the research wrong. I want you to wake up, I want you to stop being so scared. I don't know what's going on, but it can't be all that bad. The misreporting is a kind of myth building. Maybe there are temples to all the bodies we lost lining the A38. They just become so much scenery. Backdrop. Stendhal syndrome of context. In your dreams you & I are drawing Corsican Vendetta Stilettos to settle our differences. The biggest disparity is in our past. You are so intent on reclaiming it where I prefer to relive it. The papers having colluded with those paid to make sense of all our damage, confused reality with metaphor again & are recalcitrant of our history, redacting the part where they had us die & hoping instead, they start reporting how we lived.

Poem in Which My Ex's New Partner Approaches Me to Help Them Write Marriage Vows.

Sexy slenderman gangbanged in abandoned hospitals by father figures
I ejaculate loudly in an empty home
amateur condemned houses (POV) in interracial fucking
I switch my longing to guilt mode & mea culpa my sorrys for objectification
post-apocalyptic conjoined redhead twins stuck in a fridge.
this time I really mean it, my post nut clarity wins the Palme d'or
mirror twinks, slowly peel back the skin from their bones as the other gets his
guts sucked from his body by amateur pool filter.
the following day I'm stuck in traffic
echo of dead friends trapped in student debt solo size queen squirt fest
ahead a grisly accident I cannot possibly fantasise about
brutalist architecture defunded by police (roleplay)
even knowing it's a thick hot 18-wheeler & a MILF in a people carrier.
stepbrother apologising for the trauma caused in childhood
coming to my senses I mourn the wound the world made of my body
genuinely in love couple captured on SECRET cams sewn into their skin
I hear sharks have been sighted off the street we said we'd live on.
forced to watch - exes holding hands with each other & laughing
the truth is worse, it wasn't their new partner but them
everyone I have ever loved is getting creampied or pregnant or fisted or loved
unconditionally or married or having their ass eaten or loved in the way they
deserve by someone I could never be & that's just fine
You're doing better now, where I'm caught wondering if bodies define holding
hand holding with a short northern girl (ASMR)
I lose myself to horizons, select a fresh tragedy to wank over
you calling me by my name
I am searching for you in unwanted places. I won't be surprised when this
repeats itself.

Wound Detail

I have been kept awake wondering if accent is defined by body
whilst kissing like divorcees. Basking sharks, irreparable
fractures & oil slick cormorants have all been sighted
off the street we once said we would live on. Knowing others
may offer you better dreaming patterns is a kingdom of want
lost to the flood. I loved you in the wake of seas claiming the land.
When you dragged me to yet another addict festival,
the three beautiful daughters of the doctor whose life we ruined
arranged to renovate our dream home in our absence. They claimed
it was recompense for the malpractice of our bodies becoming anchors.
For their father who told us we could not breathe underwater.
For the refusal of history to relent its closure. I crave this
generous a revenge for all my unrequited drownings. But still want to
shallow our graves to protest this misdiagnosis, calm the chest of its horses
 & give in to the indulgence of mapping skin. Instead, I wreck
the sleep of history with context. Sour torsos with longing &
set unsustainable precedents for coastline paradoxes like us.
My ribs are revetments guarding my heart against scour. The scar isn't fluent
in the tide's dialect. Everything we built refuses to believe
in its own collapse & craves to be unburdened by sleep & mourning
one another & in our absence, develops a fear of drowning.

LIVES OF BRITISH SHREWS

SOREX: araneus prowling microtian muck-maze   undergrass root-tunnel
creeping with crawlers   blind writhers   lit   by vomeronasal and ultrasound
echolocation   eeek-eeek-eeek-eeek-eeek   earthworm cranefly woodlouse   *BITE*
   great indian rhino   crashing after tigers
   through the elephant grass terai   ripping
   in the softgut navel   hollowing him out
under caul-fat frettage of fan-vault grass-caves   minutus flails meat-seeking vibrissae
fibreoptic face-wands shorting and sparking   in the aurae of harvestmen   the haloes of
spiders   the electrical fields of hook-footed centipedes   and jaw-horned stagbeets
sinking her thirty-two oligocene daggers   in the proto-flesh and haemolymph   of the
cambrian arthropoda
   dead field mouse tidal   on the riding bier of self
   borne on the black and scarlet backs
   of nicrophorus vespilloides
neomys plunging sheath of silver   shattering shoals of three-spined stickleback
snipping the pincers of white-clawed crayfish   the armoured elytra   of dytiscus
marginalis   wringing out its moleskin pelt   in the skin-tight sub-sod burrow
PHOBETOR: *owl what is an owl   sudden soft night wind   notching his ear and bowling*
me over   buried alive in the ash bole larder   with the hyphae of cramp balls and emerald
borer   gulped down by squeakers   or ground to dust and   fed to babes in titmilk
   a human is shoes vibration shadow   stink
   we flee   is it shrieking or screaming   midge
   or mosquito   little ghost grass pig squealing   no?
garden tiger   needle teeth   lining them up between the mint beds   on mr & mrs turners doorstep
where frank now sits in vest and braces   wreathed in pipe smoke   pint mug steaming
as they scuttle between his carpet slippers   did he tempt them with whiskas   piglets stiffen
in daybreak dew   pale bellies still yielding   thats where we get in   when he slings them
into the mint beds   and one was a little stiff ghost
   big black water boar   up on his
   hindlegs   roaring his megahertz   gone
   amoebic floater in the pinprick pupil
jivaro shaman travelling the grass groves   hunting blindworms and wood mice   leopard slugs
pelted in slime ayahuasca   eel pursues in murky waters   impale him through the fontanelle
shrinking his head   shrinking his dreaming   his ever-expanding mind
GRASSHRIEK: two prowl the decomp labyrinths   the venomous beast of water
me   some say also the little people   but they are nothing but whiffs and glimpses
the invisible patter of inaudible footsteps   also microtis   sharp chisels soft underbelly
   clear the streets o ye squeaks
   my women will devour you   my penis is
   a hyperextended filamentous coil
but mostly me   stand back in amazement   rear like an angry or curious fitch
eeek-eeek-eeek-eeek-eeek   flee or evade   sometimes fight   but rarely to the death

when the sow is in season   earthworms are scarce   he is weak diseased or ailing
then my thirty-two razors already tear in at the throat   eeek-eeek-eeek-eeek-eeek
    teeth gripping her skull-fur
    hyperextended uncoiled penis
    deep in furnace sweetmeats
trapped in a hedge-bottom northern dairies milk bottle   his claws could not find
traction   enter the black beast   eeek-eeek-eeek-eeek-eeek   they found his fossil
inside his fossil   with the fossils of wood mice bank voles ghosts   beige slugs
algae earwigs spiders
SYSTOLE/DIASTOLE: *installed the heart from a scissor-billed hummingbird and ran it*
through the gears   eighty from cold   to one thousand two hundred   jammed into the red
meanwhile   my auditory ossicle is disintegrating   in the infrasonic assault of
    september is the cruellest month   the subsoil
    cement   worms coiled around the core   and this years
    furious soricine mouths   my poor old bones
sperm whales cycling in the range of four to eight heartbeats per minute   the lives of homeotherms
are measured in beats until the pump gives out   every species has the same identical number
it is x to the power of n   metabolic rates dictate the discharge   hence shrews live a year
    dead or catatonic on the packed earth path
    cute as a sleeping pixie   picked up and pocketed by lovely little girls
    cloakroom windows   clotted with blowflies
humans threescore and ten   sperm whales five hundred   unless they rot from anthropogenic
cancers   or are devoured by the colossal squid   which has three hearts   but whose life
is as araneus   merely an annual   like robins or sunflowers   cultureless erotic tools   designed
solely to implement   the pointedly pointless transmission of dna   which the evidence suggests
is nevertheless of the utmost importance   implying a teleology   transcending killing and sex
EROS: we could be nursed in a temperature-controlled tank of sawdust &
mealworms   and thus gain an extra year   at most   but how then would we be
wolverines or tigers   the little ones haunt us   the big ones loom   and dangle us
by our tails
    loam and leaf litter   the liminal layer
    between troposphere and topsoil
    terrorcline
four horsemen of the tangle grass arena   lawnmower   strimmer   bulldozer   fire
all their muck bunkers in vain   total body disruption with hedgehog and land eel
beheading with bufo   burial alive with smooth newt and grass snake   and
rapture to carbons with field mouse and skylark and pipit and bank vole and partridge
and whitethroat   the incinerate stump of the prophetic chickadee   zi-zi taah taah taah
    the scorpion tail of the devils coachman
    the poison mouldwarp   chafers tapeworms
    woodcock probing   dogshit
all we ask is to be horribly slaughtered and also to horribly slaughter   to stiff
and be stiffened with semen   to drop piglets   suckle and sometimes eat
them   but all being well   caravan them to killing   in the time of dearth and parricidal

competition   they will surely starve and devour us   for all you know
these little lives are sacraments & psalms   and the wind that afflates us—
THE BLUE FULMAR: *brought back from black by a teat pipette and a seven percent*
glucose solution   there was a light   a twittering voice there thinly   come to the light
little sorex   little sorex   come to the light   and the light was the brilliant liquid blackness
of the googolplexian pinhead eyes   of the soricine pleroma   dark sparks of the star
we rode as spores   from abyssal camelopardalis

    blue fulmar   cuts the turning tilth   unfurrowing squids
    and leatherjackets   froglets   leptocephali
    pink quivering nest of naked   chiasmodon niger

one hour after the glucose solution   and nine grammes of live mealworms   we are released onto
the cracked earth to die catatonic with the less insectivora   in truth we barely notice   it is like
eating the liver   of the blue fulmar

    the evolutionary level above sorex
    is homo   rejoice

    just rejoice at that shrews

or licking the endogenous dmt from sapiental cerebrospinal fluid   they can be induced to release
it by means of intraspecific violence   otherwise the entry point is the easily hollowed-out ear
like sorex they have two   like the handles of the fa cup or the greater white-toothed house shrew
enigmatic etruscans   materialised like bug-eyed ghosts   from the hepatic cells   of
the blue fulmar

EXTERMINATE THEM ALL: alternatively   the lives of british slugs
their deaths that is   the little beige garden slug   *deroceras agreste*   wet sack of gooey
protein   pumped with lappish reindeer piss   how they love henbane
ignoring the succulent soporific lettuce   to ride the edge of the cut-throat razor
to ride the blue fulmar   to die   to ride the black   blue fulmar

    stiff winging the updraft   at the cliff-top by da nizz
    right into the leicas   of the vertiginous
    elbow-propped birder

blent on the horns of the unhewn uterus   the annihilating shock of bliss   because
otherwise she would kill him   because   otherwise he would not risk death
blue fulmar   crack between the worlds

    twitching armina   geirfuglasker and funk
    spitzmausfreidareys   ledged with auks and stinking fulmars
    white savages crazed on cockspur

killing the black slug is like killing a black bear   eating the black slug is like eating
a binbag swollen with pus   these are the ways of the terracline   the mores and folk
ways   of the lower orders   just fucking kill them
TIRESIAS OF THE WRINKLED DUGS: *ecstatic liberation into analogues of death*
shrew that apparently seeks to survive   in order to pass on its troglodyte template   knows nothing
of specific teleology   but feels it in his cells like hunger   and therefore needs persuading   a bribe
inducement   quid pro quo   or maybe just a druggy buzz   blue orchid blue fulmar blue
yonder   waking to terraclines blood red dawn   xanthippe scammed and quick with
shrewlets   whats her motivation

September

Iceland, Her Touch of America

She did not whisper her winds—
she traversed them clutching

onto my steps—slowing my pace,
focusing my eyes to her frozen

tundra. My time with her, sunset
to sunrise, watching her fingers

find a brush—painting yellow
gleaming strokes against dark

canvas sky. Her snow swirls, floating
waves pulling as river's undertow—

waist deep—an ice ocean wasteland,
feeling of isolation, crystalizing

camera images, crackling skin,
cold cutting through seams

of layered clothes. She warned me
of the America I would find leaving her.

Nine Months in Midwest Wheat Country—

amber grains wave in Des Moines, silence
the s—the monks have left. Just above
poor-trash-class life, south-side, struggling.
America. Our neighbor accepted us,

we play his Mattel's Intellivision
video game. Watch him run outside
to grab softball size hail, storming
winds in circles, innings of pitches
from the sky. We listen to Music
Television's birth: "Video Killed
the Radio Star," "In the Air Tonight,"
"Stop Draggin' My Heart Around,"

"Whip it." We went scrapping
for spare change, cutting grass,
collecting glass bottles. Joy riding,
jumping bikes in hilly dunes,
four-wheelers across sandy dunes,
jeeps in curvy dunes—hanging on
to jeep rails as the jeep rolls over—night joy
finds us tipping tired cows over—
hiding in shadows from angry farmers.

My voice places me in speech classes
so my American teacher can understand
my English accent. Not sure if I got picked
on being black, sounding different,
or not being American when a car passed
our car with a sign, *"Niggers kiss ass"*,
squeezing ass cheeks against passenger
window. Amber grains wave us away.

Chess Piece Patterns

I was never taught how to play
chess. At seven, I watched

my uncle position-play his friends
after his Amway presentations.

Dimensions of strategy, stretching
my mind six moves ahead

with pyramid impact, knotted
in my memory. I learned

most people I met repeated
movements, chess pieces

within safe parameters, recurring
pawns and rooks, looped

by a yarn of life's conditions,
compelled by fear, failure—running

when others were running
without hearing the gunshots

others heard at a Miami Bass
concert. A girl is laughing

loving a boy in our high school
locker room—a train of six

boys follows. I blend
hidden against a dark corner.

Autumn Love Poem

She was coughing again
last night, I couldn't sleep

and sat at our table,
nervous in the moonlight.

Something at the window
was trying to get in,

the moon looked right through me
and made a hollow sound.

The moon once sang and danced,
once told the greatest jokes;

my girl laughed for ever,
my girl and I both laughed.

I'll make some soup, good soup,
stir honey in her tea.

Her clothes hang loose, slip down.
She filled them in the spring.

Space

It's not true that people like me.
OK, it's true sometimes
but mostly not. They don't like me
and I often can't stand the sight of them.

To be with my wife is enough for me,
just to occupy the same space.

She's engrossed in *The Invasion*
which is, she claims, a cracking read
about the gentrification of working class areas.

What gets her most is the indifference.
I think at times that gets me most as well.
Times like today, yesterday, tomorrow.

If

If all music sounded like the world's angriest hornet amplified a thousand times

and if "wheat" did not appear on every packet in our kitchen but "trilby" and "vest" did

and if 'My Funeral' was a popular name for a girl

and if dodos weren't extinct but sailors were

and if magpies recited poems in the voice of Noel Coward

and if David Icke was wrong about the lizards

and if Captain Kirk and Mister Spock materialised every time you looked in your wardrobe

and if a cat running up a curtain was the basis for the world's most popular religion

and if Picasso had died a virgin in a house full of tears

and if people bought so many books they had nowhere to put them

and if pork pies and tobacco turned out in the end to be good for you

and if all the stupid films were brilliant films

and if the Marx Brothers had been called the Hitler Brothers and their reputation had waned

and if thoughts and ideas weren't lost if you didn't note them but waited for you in the fridge

and if the Prime Minister replied to questions with harmonica solos

and if the moon landings had never happened, or had

and if there was more than one way to outrun a lion

and if the strings of your heart could not be plucked

and if we encountered the under toad at an early age and knew when he was coming every time

and if Professor Hard Times and Joe Ignorant were the Trotsky and Stalin of British politics

and if 'Once Upon a Time in the West' was set in the East

and if everybody had size fourteen feet

and if a cat running up a curtain was a vital clue

and if the Queen published a lurid sex manual

and if an old school tie was merely something you used to choke a bastard

and if we all had to hide in a foreign embassy for ever knitting patterned pullovers

and if coming second was better than coming first

and if it was only possible to speak in the present tense

and if no one could ever miss a bus, or catch an undertone

and if people working in fish 'n' chip shops were better off than lawyers

and if you could stare at a boot and find something in it and not just a foot

and if we were immortal and God was an abandoned pizza with a cigarette crushed out in

      the crust

and if people still had lives rather than gadgets

and if Tarring Neville was not a village but a procedure

and if Peter, Paul and Mary had been called Dick, Balls and Quim

and if no one spent their life looking for stuff to sniff at

and if *Beat the Devil* was not a movie liked only by phonies et moi

and if kicking against the pricks was a degree course at Oxford and Cambridge

and if President Oscar Flake made smoking marijuana compulsory

and if a postcard from the seaside was a portent of doom

and if the world's most venomous snake was a pacifist

and if a cat running up a curtain was a cure for cancer

and if the greatest minds of our time all chose television game shows as a career

and if birds could only fly backwards and were constantly colliding comically

and if ashtrays could be used to replace diseased lungs

and if bicycles were poems and saddlebags field recordings

and if game birds enjoyed being blown to bits in mid-flight

and if you always got a good night's sleep no matter what

and if investment bankers always spoke with their fingers stretching each side of their mouth

and if Malcolm X had been white and Bob Dylan had been black and still only one had
          survived the 60s

and if Thelonious Monk was still gigging at the Five Spot

and if one and one made boo and boo and boo made boo hoo

and if something bit you on the leg every time you travelled by train

and if hamsters surprised us by saving the planet

and if the ghosts of Frank Zappa and Bill Hicks were running on the Republican ticket

and if Vincent Price and his mother were there to greet us at the gates of Paradise

and if a cat running up a curtain was an ingredient in a pie

and if the lines of a poem could be read in any order

and if it was impossible to run out of steam

and if the second world war had been a hen party

then maybe this would be the nation's favourite poem.

deluge

wellspring
  of seed
Noah saved
   in the brimful ark
     the wolvene
     the kyne
all the nobility of beast
the silken worm best
  of all
plus the pigs
  those pearly-queens
the diminutive-souled giraffes
the carry-castles the heath-cats
sailing past all dangers
   the three pestilences of the reign of Edward III
   the raging-about of the water-newts from stem to stern
   the lurking places of the Semi-Saxons
until the dovene sprang up
to silence the owl and slay her stepfather not once but thrice

Noah Theatre

Now let the Water-Carriers come forth
to perform the play of Noah and the Fludde
Let them mum how "*The flood comes in fleeting fast;*
On every side it spreadeth full fare;
Let them play the carrying in of provisions
and the entry of the animals, bears and ants,
monkeys, mice and marmosets, etc.
Let he who plays Noah with beard of goosequills shout loudly –
For fear of drowning I am agast; Good gossip, let us draw near.
Let he who playeth Noah's Wife mock all women
gossiping in bonnet and shawl
boozing and making merry with her friends
spurning the saviour Ark
and let he who plays Shem also demean all women
as on Father Noah's orders
he seizes his mother with no respect and carries her raging
(how we all laugh) into the Ark
forcing her from her home and all she holds dear and familiar,
her household, her kitchen clean as a knife blade,
her embroidered linen, vegetable beds ready for harvest,
tearing her away on a mere promise from god
who has never spoken a word to her,
taken into exile because of a stupid hunch her old man had about the weather.

family life

Shem, Ham and Japheth
side with sun
moon and stars

sons who'll owe their lives
to the boon
of light tipped over
our pardoned earth

sons who bring Noah
the ready cup of broth
a dose of aardwolf spit and valerian

(heard ye his wild psalming in spell-time of night?)

Noah hun drink this calmdown cup
of whitherso and why
brewed by your serious sons

ark builders who bring you back to yourself
whenever you get lost in the holy of holies
while your three daughters-in-law
sell your shoes to the air

splish splash
hoist your spirits sky-high
on a rattly rope of cobra fangs
plait your beard like a bus driver's and fix it with a loom band

trim those backsliding toenails
tazer you with kisses from here to Mount Ararat
as is writ in the Book of Jubilees

decorative

your vulnerability is that you are a joke

you know you are a bruised peach

you can pinpoint the date and time it all began

you fear anyone who meets you now will know

you want to slip inside cool water

you will let him destroy you then wake up the next day

and do his dishes

you say okay and fine after saying no a thousand times

you realise this isn't what consensual means

you throw up

you think if you could bite into your bones they'd crunch like an apple, not a nectarine

you want people to belong together

you belong to every man who has ever touched you

you realise love has an edge

you'll never have sex again

your thoughts will outlive you

you think souls exist but have nothing to do with morality

and everything to do with cool water

heaven is conditional

you decide to like people depending on whether they accept your friend requests

you realise women are a metaphor and faking it

means you've never been loved

a shadow of it

maybe –

eating unsliced cucumber is an anarchist act

don't you think? I ask, slicing the pointed green tip
we're in a time of no sex but
half an hour before
we'd pressed against one another
all breath and hunger
you're barely listening
an artistic act? you repeat
can you cut me two slices?
tenderly, I slice two concentric slithers –
half-moons – promise myself:
this is not a metaphor
I know we're going to end but I don't know when
I think we're going to end or else
we'll continue in circles forever
the cucumber waits on the chopping board
in a pool of its own secretions
thinking death has surely met it
is it not tiring always thinking about cucumbers
and anarchism, like you're some kind of fucking
vegetable missionary? I want you to say
are you not exhausted, feasting on diluted pulp,
expecting fulfilment?
I want to pick up the cucumber and shove it so far down my throat I choke
I wonder if you'd laugh or even look up
I wonder if it'd turn you on
who is looking at me while I look at this cucumber?
pathetic, parted from its head, pooled in its own wet
in a few years this will all make sense
in a few years there will be no proof this dead thing existed
for now, the cucumber waits
begging for disorder
I lift its willing body to my mouth
let my teeth grate a hole in the silence
I wonder what rot will find it first

I don't know how to tell you this

but I'm white cold like that too-late sensation of leaning over the draining board and realising all the knives are facing blade-up. I'm sweet and my mouth is filled with quicksand muscovado, tongue thumbing the graves of my empty gums. In the pit of my stomach lives an eclipsing sun. I step around the blind corner into oncoming traffic. I am the concrete smack of a papier-mache skull against the corner of a table-top. I am that moment at the cinema where you turn to your date and say ooooh. I felt that. I am a curling toe. The phantom hammer hitting your kneecap. As the blunt metal makes contact - I am a thousand standing court room ovations. I am the crunch of a snail's shell in the morning when you're outside bare foot. The avocado stone hitting the floor - green flesh splatter. I'm the moment at the threshold, knowing. I am the final warning, eviction-notice red font. I am the nail varnish chipping as the door scrapes over your foot. I am indulgent,

lick of salt on a throbbing wound.

Things you could return as:

3000 tiny gnats waiting to be swallowed

A bat, denied of flight, throwing itself from the second floor

Flying ants stripping their anniversary wings

A nest chewed through from underneath

The Tkk Tkk bird, silent for windchimes

Steel shrinking with a click

A retained bee's single house

A windmill clicking

Poe's birds vocal tennis

A raised wolf announcing itself

Bonfire fresh in midnight air

The stream and the Tkk Tkk bird in harmony

Things you do return as:

Muzzled static

Grief spread across sleep

Tsunami winds

Dreams to ghost and haunt

Year After Year Onwards
Epilogue

We make our way to morning,
in the corner of the field a nest,
an egg in its throat,
the TKK TKK bird's gallbladder intact.

An Eastern Imperial flies at tree level
as we walk up and down,
a hole in a carrier bag,
your ashes everywhere but here.

This early light is still
bright orange as in a painting
from a time before time,
not forgotten but a mystery

We are in the mud and stones
of the river as somewhere
the day and the dark
meld into one another like time

And then I am in the nest.
The stream is a river,
the mud looks like an ocean.
You are on the banks.

You are in the river, crowing,
heading out to sea once more.
You are reborn, boundless,
a jellyfish again and again.

You are on the river,
with your mother and grandmother
and the water that never stops
to be held with these hands.

The sky and the sea,
the stones and the stars
And you, everywhere,
a crow in a nest catching worms.

It is too difficult to hold this world
in the palms of our hands.
Can we live together today
and die together once more?

'Can birds do what they like?'
after Brian and Charles (2022)

The second-hand keyboard is patient,
A poor dentistry of smiles that knows the peril

Of local ambition from its makeshift perch on the sill.
The stand is with a writer. It's not mine

Yet. The little robot I borrowed makes sound
From sound, and walks along to Ornithology.

It imitates. It is an imitator. It is a cheap instrument
Like a washing machine for a stomach.

Like gloves for hands. Like your grandmother's curtains
I fashion for a dress. Or my first trip to the shops

For milk, old man in shoes, face like a found object
Whose repurposing makes a parent worried sick.

I play with automatic hand and think on the upward stair
Of you, like a banister at the contour of its spiral.

It's nice here. Tree outside the window. Dictionary at the door.
Playing pretend the lightning strike's amateur scientist.

You can call me Charles, if you like. It's the likeness that does
 it. He sounds just like a real person.

In the House that Jack Built

there once was a shoe. foom-tchee foom-tchee. the shoe is there. foom-tchee foom-tchee. there once was a shoe that belongs to a foot, that foot is mine. foom-tchee foom-tchee. the shape of the foot. foom-tchee foom-tchee. has a gum and a tongue. foom-tchee foom-tchee. the shape of the foot has a gum and a tongue, is one foot long. foom-tchee foom-tchee. the length of the tongue. foom-tchee foom-tchee. is one foot long. foom-tchee foom-tchee. the length of the room on the length of the tongue is one foot long. foom-tchee foom-tchee. the tongue is yours. foom-tchee foom-tchee. the room's mine. foom-tchee foom-tchee. the love in the room at the foot of the bed by the shoes is ours. foom-tchee foom-tchee. the shoes are off. foom-tchee foom-tchee. it's three o'clock. foom-tchee foom-tchee. the shoes that are off with the tongue hanging out are open, unlaced. foom-tchee foom-tchee. here are the socks. foom-tchee foom-tchee. the shoes are sick. foom-tchee foom-tchee. the shoes that are sick and the socks that are hid in the shape of the shoe with the gum and the tongue that is one foot long are quietly rocked in the arms of the clock as the night peters out through the room, the room, the room, as night peters out through the room

Baddies
after the MGM slogan

It should be said for the sake of it
There is no better reason I think
For thoughts to make a break for it
Like convicts from Her Maj's clink

My only hope's they're sympathetic
An Eastwood, Clooney, Pitt or Caine
The loquacious gangster's copacetic
That gives the slip the lawman's chain

Or said not seen, the greatest heist
That springs the mind's own Alcatraz
And steals away the thoughts we diced
With cell-block tango razzmatazz

This sleight of hand is our diversion
It breaks the rules but keeps the line
And dupes surveilling self-aversion
To think each passing thought is fine

For when we judge, we jail, are jailed
These sentences commit offence
They section us where none are bailed
Their terms betray our innocence

October

I

He speaks to the water / In the third-floor lavatory of
the flooding gallery / he lowers his lips to the basin / It listens
/ renders his messages in tongues no one can untangle /
The louder his secrets / the safer it keeps them / When
he stops / the reflection stirs to a blur / eyes trembling
like a room in translation / Now another man is staring at him
/ melting / necktie hanging like a flap of skin / a clue of red
cloud / diffusing through the water in a drunken sunset /
He tries to walk out of this strange life / and slips into a mirror

II

A skull missing from the body of an unnamed man /
Every night he sinks in the quiet / waiting till the darkness
squeezes him into scenes he can never escape from / rooms in
old homes visited by everyday ghosts / His father rocks
in an armchair with the cleaner kneeling between his legs /
praying / inaudibly / eyes turned glass / while in the next room
a woman is holding the telephone with the low drone
of the sea in her ear / Somewhere down the corridor / the
red man is trying to run away / but his legs are caught
in the tenderness of water / The house will hang him
on the walls like another still life / They'll never find him now

III

There he is / hauling the boy out of the river and lighting up his eyes again / *I'm sorry it took you and not me* / *Love is a junkyard of toys* / *This is a dream* / *of course* / *so you need to go back when it's over* / *Till then* / *I'll carry you like a wound* / And they pass through the trees / filling each other's lips with the same blood memories / At the bridge / they spill into a pop song / taken over by cannons and trumpets till the light rises / and the boy / falling in another war /is taken by the red water / brushed to the sea

Carotid Artery I Can Hear the Sea

I never saw it written down, only heard
it in Silent Witness during an autopsy. I
imagined   it   a   thing   having
happened,   heard   'carotted'
like   'garrotted,'   'corrected'
or   'corroded';   a   cause   of
death   a   mistake   a
contributing factor not just a part,
named. A teacher, later, corrected a
title to capitalise the 'I' of 'is'; I hadn't
known that 'is' was a verb, that just
being, now, was enough to qualify
as an action. You're doing it right
now, oxygen-rich blood passing this
verb unchallenged into your head,
face, brain. Feel them, call it
sound if you like: The paths
of   two   narrow
misunderstandings   either   side
of a windpipe.

People Just Add Something;
This Time the Thing Is a Mole

I went to Enid's funeral and there was a mole on the coffin and it seemed aware of us but unconcerned. Also—and not to underplay this—the seats were made of moles and everyone there was a mole. After, I shook their clawed hands as best I could and they said Fee you are the great-niece who is always talking about moles! It struck me as odd how earlier they must have paid someone to dig the big hole with spades.

Now around six months later all the mole hills fall flat at once, bespoke sinkholes calculated perfectly by a podium of child geniuses. I think of Debbie and her daughter calling to one another on the eventless, minimally reactive surface of the earth, low VOCs. Things are repainted. The moles have all gone. Maxim walks the new flatness complaining how in films the gravestone is always erected too soon.

Reliable Witnesses

After the ancient Roman sculpture of Pan and the nanny goat (in marble)

I used to know this guy who claimed
                              convincingly
on a night out
that in an unaccounted few moments
                    on a small street
the Greek god Pan came to him and said

        don't be such a bloody idiot

but Pan (who has sex with goats while
              Paparazzi sculptors chip on)
                                    can't talk

while being a great role model and
                    (look at it going in)
a great nude model
and a goatfucker and
                    very possibly
someone's idea of a bloody idiot.

I wonder if he was *intimidated*
I wonder what happened to that guy I knew,
if he:

      moved away or

      took up with sculptors or

      kept on in the admin job —

Missing Person

I was a convict boy who dreamed of running.
No surprise that the men who had
got my attention. It was on a job near Heathrow,

driven out to a verge in a minibus
crammed with my fellow have-nots. We were hefting mulch
around sapling trees, squinting in the gale force

draft from the haulage trucks, when I found the bag.
Like looking at a corpse, the three of us
stood and stared. Big enough to hold a body,

the weight of a life. *You unzip it. No, you.* I pulled slowly,
like defusing a bomb. The payload damp and rife with mould.
We found a bunch of keys. Socks, boots, shorts, and jeans.

And a brand new pair of shoes, which the lad from Stockport took,
along with a watch that had no strap. We rummaged in the pockets
for money. Nothing but a Polaroid

soldier in the wild, smiling for the lens in his camo gear. We studied
his face for clues. Of what, God knows. Then we got back to work.
I'm not sure about the other two, shovelling

shit on minimum wage, but I was jealous. Here was a man
who'd stepped from his skin, scrubbing out a name and starting again.
Dead or alive. I wonder if he hears the traffic

like I still do, rattling a soul from a ribcage. Or how the airport
booms with soaring jets, the wing tips
trimmed with light.

Mowde Bush Stone

Take the gravel track out past the tumbledown farm
where time is folding in on itself, as if the unlikely

beginnings of a black hole crumpling space
through an old slate roof, avoiding the dead end lane

where doggers and smokers hide from the world with weed
or sex, and then climb the padlocked gate rusted

fast to a concrete post, you'll see a six-foot stone
in the corner of a meadow. This is not the polished monolith

humming with an alien missive. It's a lump of rock
in a deep green field, given meaning by druids and witches,

hippies and frauds, and once worshipped by Victorian mystics
who may have also picked the liberty cap mushrooms

on the Saxon ridge. I like to think, when the psilocybin hit,
that they lay for a while with the flowers and the sky,

watching bees track pollen from petal to petal,
before the universe wall gave way.

Dorothy

With her little dog woofing at the woman
on a broom, and a house in flight on a thunderhead
twist of Kansas dirt, I'm Dorothy in spirit
in a campsite storm.

And if the world is left when I wake here
tomorrow, and the caravan has held
to a windblown field
where the stars unhinge from a cosmic wall,

I want the ruby red shoes
and a yellow brick road, not the deckchair wreckage
in a tree by the gate, clanging on a post
like a doom-chime bell.

I want the Technicolor walk
in the opioid dell, the little blue river
in a plastic town where the munchkins chuckle
with a merry old witch. Put me in Oz

while the news is on, where the Taliban trend
and the Red Woods burn. I'll see a bat-winged
chimp and have no fear, leaning on
a friend of gleaming tin.

Leave the wizard alone, let him draw the curtain
and keep on working. He's busy with sky
and puffs of cloud. The polychromic
burst of curving light.

cyn

aileni'r lôn dan olwynion, cyn i'r haul
adael olion ei ddychwelyd, cyn chwalu'r
ysbrydion o'r landin, cyn rhedeg dŵr,
cyn llosgi'r croen â mân ddefodau'r dydd;
cyn dwyn diniweitrwydd y gwlith, cyn datod
petalau, cyn saernïo paned, cyn poeni,
cyn tywallt poteli, cyn gweddi, cyn gwaedd
a chyn deall meidroldeb pob golau newydd,
dyma ti. Dyma ti, mor noeth â dydd dy eni,
yn lledu dy lygaid trwy'r porffor dwfn,
yn agor dy ddwylo hyd gilfachau'r tŷ,
yn tyfu'n anferth yn y llonydd anorffenedig,
yn bwrw gwreiddiau i'r distiau astud

yn dechrau anghofio'r wyrth o ddeffro, yn barod.

before

the road is reborn under tyres, before the sun
leaves the marks of its returning, before ghosts
disperse from the landing, before taps are turned,
before the skin burns with the day's small devotions,
before the morning's dewy innocence is stolen, before
petals are undone, before coffee, before worry,
before bottles smash in bins, before prayers, before screams,
and before understanding the finiteness of all new light,
here you are. Here you are, bare as the day you were born,
stretching your eyes through the deep purple,
opening out your hands into the recesses of this house,
growing huge in this unfinished silence,
casting roots into the dropping eaves

beginning to forget the miracle of awakening, already.

stafelloedd amhenodol

Yr hyn sy'n aros o hyd yw'r aros, y bobl na chofiaf
eu hwynebau – dim ond eu tymer a'u hystum;
eu haflonyddu a'u llonyddu drachefn, eu siffrwd
a'u mân siarad, eu beiros gwag a'u hembaras.

Pobl fel chdi a fi, yn hanner-byw mewn gofodau
diduedd o olau, a'r dyddiau'n eu gwelwi;
pobl sy'n disgwyl am i rywun alw'u henwau
heb wylio'r waliau rhag eu gweld yn dynesu

heb wylio'r waliau rhag ofn nad ydynt yno,
rhag i'r muriau cadarn droi'n llenni o'n cwmpas,
rhag i'r gwynt ddod ar garlam i rwygo'r ffabrig
a'n gadael yn noeth mewn anadliad lle bu stafell

lle bu syniad am neuadd o gorneli perffaith
i gael trefn ar ein sypiau esgyrn ac eistedd i aros.

rooms: unspecified

What always remains for me is the waiting itself, the people
whose faces I never remember – only their temper and poise,
their fidgeting and settling, their shufflings
and mutterings, their empty biros and embarrassment.

People like you and I, half-living their lives in impartially
lighted spaces, getting paler with each day,
people waiting for someone to call their names
not watching the walls lest they should come closer

not watching the walls lest they should not be there,
lest the stones should become curtains around us,
lest the wind should gallop through, ripping the fabric
leaving us naked in a breath that was once a room

where once was an idea for a hall of perfect corners
to arrange our bundles of bones and sit to wait.

Vertigo

for once
make real the curse
you prophesy
not-knowing
distance nor
consequences

fearing less
what's below
than the heights
unconquered

gravity   unfurl!

saturated with vain
mondanités   utterly
insolvent   reliant on
a lover's alms

embracing downwardness

o this little twitch I give
just before hitting the
ground

visceral contusion

will *not*
for once
wake upon
arrival

on you thick pile of dead
leaves   promise of
salvation

m   e   a   n   d   e   r

Just like a snake I crave the burn the summer traces on my skin on every glimpse the sun may seize of it as it peels away and the new delays its thickening—despite a certain swelling thirst and a sane amount of wariness. As we walk on the sunny side at snail pace and trail our sugarcoated legs and slime, my ankles turn relentlessly. *Would we hold hands, would we, if we were sure to get it back afterwards*? No. Now: isn't this bus stop a safe place, a haven for poultry's remains where I shall pompously declare: *Communism looks good on you* (even though your faith has faded). Spit—thrown off bridges and balustrades, travels by means of gravity, through time, and sometimes hangs in mid-air, defying expectancy. When you say *I love you*, I say *of course, who wouldn't*, betraying disbelief. Shade—in woodlands, shed its flattering light shyly on one side of your face, hiding rings and wrinkles. The B-side of mine grinds against the rocks and the eyes go milky; erosion scatters our scales around. Stray dogs follow us to the cliff edge in a crocodile line until we run out of food

Accolade

I go to the bathroom for quick relief
but the door is made of glass and does not
lock. I am wholly naked when a two year-old
already acting like a biped enters the flat using
his own set of keys. We embrace. I inquire about
his day. He went to the swimming pool, he says.
I confess my envy. What incredible independence,
eloquence, at such a young age. I can talk about
anything with my boy!
Now sitting on the rocking chair by the window
giving onto grey empty streets depicted with
straight lines and smooth surfaces, all stainless
steel-like. I am holding him near my heart.
We are both naked but his skin
is warmer than mine

church in the woods

I stand outside the cathedral   which was wooded
once   helicopters gull over

the gardener's bonnet   soundynge emergency
mid-century gothic signage   as if god

was a typographer   helle-fearynge peasants
worked here for free   before evensong

poverty stays in the soil like sanctity   *the parish church*
was known   *as the church in the woods*

unseasonable warmth   acer leaves brownynge
the Clean Air Zone   weathercock still

as a severed tongue   carpark clouded with National
Trust stickers   I used to enter every church I passed

the word itself steepled with aitches
now I'm apathetic   uninterested in powers

that revoke love in the blink   of a sun
tithe barns full of tongues   dry as controlled demolition

I sit on a dark wooden bench in the autumnal yard
opposite   the de Lacy community centre

the paradox of tonguelessness is voice
what is our common   condition now

demesne

compare with *domain*   meanynge
this land is not yrs

there are implications to exclusion
take this field

skin flappynge
from my gaol shredded

by barbed wire   durynge
   recreational activity

take this duchy   thynges more covert
than flesh

generatynge revenue for kyng
or quene   or john of gaunt

take the ryght to destroy
never a lastynge bone

hoof

pilgrimynge to sites   you roamed
            wi flaysome hooves
   where bonnie wimmin wackered
at the sight   o your tusks

waist deep
                in hip-breear
woodgatherynge in the commons
turned brownfield sites
wells replaced wi taps   reservoirs
at lower levels
      than predicted
this dreedist somer   no reyn
you couldn't beliven here
now   the wold is fellen

no county for bristle and snaht
  they thought you   brute
    doing what they did to ahr land
wi walls wi lords and wi law

November

You mimic the posture of a kratt, born from black currants and spare farm equipment.

/

You are given a task and thus life. It is difficult to remember when you were last capable of work.

/

Labor is a privilege of the kratt-body.

/

Without labor you become unstable. Whatever scythes and rakes have been strapped together to make your body begin to vibrate and loosen.

The kratt is valued as a golem. It is in the debt of whoever has forced life upon it.

/

I do not think that we are yet in a position to reach any conclusions. But I hope that by raising these concerns, we can begin the process of reaching them (REDACTED).

/

What turned it all to disgust? Is it the mask that I'm wearing?

/

Labor → Value → Depletion → Metamorphosis

In this kratt-body you are gifted 6,000 years of work. Plowing every field in the Estonian landscape until the ground has been eradicated and there is no more crop left to grow or harvest.

/

This leaves a contusion zone like a crater—the place where all of your effort has accumulated.

/

You can only care for so long before that care becomes harm, and that harm becomes an unconcealable scar.

/

If you hear a voice speaking to you from the base of your skull. It is not you. It is your ancient reptilian brain.

/

At the base of your skull, there is an unconceable scar.

1986

Strangers call her a clever boy
fooled by green dungarees, her bald dome
are you a little big man then?
They fling him up in the air, high as he can go.
Eventually a ringlet sprouts
centre stage on her eggshell head
mum clamps it with a plastic bow
what a prettylittlething   what a sweetie.
Chomping on dirt dad slaps an earthworm
from her portly fist
the puddles are suddenly too toxic.

2016

One long synth note
signals it's the morning after a big party
wide-angle shot of the clouds (time lapse)
the flamingo tinted dawn,
close-ups on pretty sweaty faces
the effects of a pill tapering off.
On the walk home she counts
11 new flags on her road
some are Jacks, others are Georges,
a chorus of tuts, the dawn roar of the A road
a Ring doorbell reports her
for door-knocking.
In her constant quest to be an outsider
she forgets that she too
is part of the white masses,
she thinks she should talk
to more old people
(as long as they are not her parents)
to try and understand
where they are coming from,
she balances a coffee cup
on her brand-new laptop
just to feel dangerous.

2012

The world didn't end as predicted.
Flash mobs are spreading
at every station in the city
groups of grown-ups
box step, shoulder roll, clap-clap-jump!
For the finale, an attempt at a grapevine.
Is it team building?
Are they selling a new power juice?
She works at quaint festivals
making decorative tea towels with children,
only eats happy animals,
it's the wettest August on record.
She assumed she'd be in Belize
by now, or Mexico, but she's crawling
on her friend's kitchen floor
left tit hanging out her jumpsuit
acid breath singalong
with her greatest loves
women who speakerbox each other's victories,
sink quiet jealousies,
whose bodies will grow
and shrink cells of life and destruction,
spitting sav blanc
back in the mug she screams
turn up the bass bitch!

No One Said Magic
Had to Be Useful

I believe in magic
for the same reason
I am afraid of the dark;
you don't know
what you don't know
until after it has torn
your throat out.

So I found the mint
that grew into a washcloth
when watered, wildly
enchanting. Childlike,
I nearly clapped
when the rosemary oil
reached my nose.

Didn't care that
they'd laid a napkin
over my lap earlier,
that I'd already licked
my fingers fully clean,
or that any remnants
I wrapped in this white flag
to take with me would carry
with them the smell of defeat.

> Not that I expected
> any scraps to survive
> when served such
> small plates.

Ragstone

you grow hungry   appetite inflamed
the stone bowl   waiting   warm

to the touch   the spoon   hesitates
sits   for a moment   before digging

the brown foam   hides   its gold
goat cheese treasure   cool   sticky

in the warm mousse   you savour
this simple course   its eye watering

cost   the foam rich   the candied
walnuts break   under the crush

of teeth   hardened   with mercury
against   the grind   against

the poverty   weakened   by three
sugars in every tea to fight the pangs

the cost of   weekly shop expands
electricity price rises   gas

builds up   held firm   in the foam
the mousse sets   each tiny course

              fills you up slowly

John D. Rockefeller

This was unfamiliar.
I could tell it was white,
end of conversation.
I've seen food like this,
but not often enough
to intuit whether it's
cod or haddock or...

  Hake? Okay,
  if you say so.

When I look it up later
It turns out there are
thirteen distinct species
of this fish but no notes
on whether the flavour
wavers between them,
nothing about what
makes them unique,
just talk of where they
came from.

This,
this is very familiar,
I can tell, it is white
and rich.

Above Black Lake

Perhaps she is sitting somewhere

Perhaps she is wearing a heavy felt hat

Perhaps she is not there at all,
  she is not at all what we think she is

Perhaps not knowing her is better than knowing her
  or knowing her too well

Perhaps that's why she comes to this town... no, this hamlet where neighbors
  know each other by name, though it ends there

Perhaps where she can't

Perhaps with the first letter of her name, she begins... or ends... or both
  not being what she began with. This letter, so common it is, I don't recall it

Perhaps she's dressed for winter or spring. Not summer

Perhaps she prefers the cold wind she drinks down when it whips up around her

Perhaps she is an image left on a still black lake high up near the moon, or high
  up enough to take it like that high above Black Lake. Isn't that the name. Isn't that
  first letter the first letter of her name

Perhaps she's not there and we aren't. Just there, standing on a slope that
  swerves down through firs to the bank of the lake, that deep dark lake where light
  perishes soundlessly

Perhaps she's come back because she wants to, because once, here, she had an
  affair. Isn't that right? Isn't that what she wants? The sound that moves her?
  Isn't that the music in the movement that moves her?

Perhaps that's it

Perhaps that's what she thinks and feels standing on the slope that swerves to
  the bank

Perhaps she's trying not to cry

Perhaps she'd rather laugh

It's too much, too little, too quick or slow

It lingers. The affair

Perhaps she doesn't want to remember all that much about it

Perhaps she's tried to and can't

Perhaps the less it matters, the more she wants it

Perhaps she says it just like that on the slope that swerves through the firs,
    bushes, dead soggy branches, rabbit or deer spunk, those old branches covered with
    green lichen red lichen yellow lichen, the muddy bank where the tide laps and the
    sparrows dip down to sip the rich black onyx water

Perhaps, she sees herself in the water when she gets down to it

Perhaps when she gets down to it. She sees her face and doesn't recognize it

Perhaps the game she plays at Black Lake, the rich onyx water, the heavy girth
    of it swelling and rising and falling, imperceptibly, impishly, derisively...

Perhaps her felt hat, her straw hat, her sitting somewhere, her wool skirt,
    her cotton skirt, her mouth just slightly open, her hands in her lap, her eyes, her
    black onyx eyes, this deep dark girth on the slope above the bank when sparrows
    dip their heads to sip the rich water with their beaks

Perhaps you remember her

Perhaps I don't or can't however much I want to

Perhaps relieved by the simplicity and beauty of the lake, the firs,
    the girth of it swelling and falling

Perhaps that's all she wants or doesn't want to admit she wants in that way, at
    the bank bending down, cupping water in her two hands and sipping

Spring Mist Dawn

I have for several days now struggled to come to terms with my inability to sketch even briefly the vast implications that three words compel: *spring mist dawn.* Even their minutiae escape me in cliches that are better forgotten but which populate the very air we breathe, you and I. If I can find any solace at all, it comes because I have found a way to elude the stress of failure, this absence that falls to the pit of the stomach and which absorbs, slowly or quickly, what does it matter, the physical and emotional plateaus that hunger instills. And yet, drawn as I am to those words, become chalk white frescoed glyphs floating in the bluing sky – a simple image, yes, but finally an image – I listen to the music they hold within them: the hard 'g,' the near onomatopoetic sibilance that dovetails to the percussive 't,' and the final diminuendo that slightly opens its lips to whisper an end note. And from that score aerial missives strip down to their vegetal bones and silver throated Gorgons in bright red skirts powder their bristled cheeks.

Music can sometimes do this where meaning cannot. The former infecting the latter until they couple, unfazed by their differences or distinctions, happy at last to have found that intemperate dance, which marks them and us, mirrors that we are to each other.

Spring mist dawn...

The trio evanesces, the words decouple, their music lingers for as long as we hear them and then, hushed, the room carries their last vibration in 'n.'

An end.

York is a City of Marvels.

for Anthony Capildeo

I

a visitation. commencing.
with late gently. delayed.

the arrival. of pocket texts.
hastens. the anticipation.

of Anthony. of the lost hour.
in the apse. of the station.

II

at the edge. of a swathe. of shallow water.
overhung. by a sweep. of weeping willow.

a sign appears. heralding.
birds. of the campus lake.

followed. in quick succession.
by the apparition. of said birds.

having nothing. with which.
to make. an offering.

I stand. dumbstruck.
and gaze. upon them.

the Moorhen. stalks off. dowdy body.
teetering. on extravagant feet.

the mallard. expresses an enthusiasm.
disproportionate. to the situation.

of geese. there are Greylag.
Lesser Snow. and Canada.

what's good for the Gadwall.
is good for the Goosander.

of the Black Swan. no sign.
of the Mute Swan. no comment.

III

upon entering. a building.
upon entering. a room.

vapours. of white spirit.
rising. enveloping.

developing. an eye.
for a cupboard. of colours.

an affection. for a face. of type.
a feeling. for letter forms. ligaments.

fumbling. towards an understanding.
of blue. as an expectation. a thirst.

for the always. already sky.
of colonial. imagination.

squatting. to examine. drawers. of plates.
of religious themes. pastoral scenes.

objects. of advertisement.
bordering. on decoration.

a silver. of squiggles.
a thesis. of rivers.

a press. printing.
on thin ice.

December

surface audience

snow-blind bulge of water
surface helical or like a
funhouse mirror

on the hudson bay a pod of seals surround our boat
in their hundreds   i am worried the whole time in a way
i can't describe   the presence of so many heads
turned
in our direction
coming to their   polite points   and earless too
or i guess
they have
ears but
the thing about that wait is you cannot locate a word in
it   you cannot strain light through its more porous
parts   it is just a clutch of individuals knotting their fear
and the sudden sharpness of promontories
in the distance
i won't remember anything else about that day   except the
interior of a restaurant cavernous and spaceship-like   there
is always such a feeling of accelerated doubt when you put
your first foot on to a moving vessel   i always
think i can
rehearse the motion   plan for it   or calculate how much
the waves would plunge at a greater speed   so those
first few
seconds are horrible

Unspeak

For this one, there is   no   reframed sentence;
there is no contingency plan. Your departure
is an endpoint that has threatened to swallow
me with its silver tide for   as   long as   sips and
suns and sand. For as long as   flame-coloured
roses have existed, as long as rock   has pressed itself in layers
by the coast here, the marram grass   flocked   with stars.
Everything holding its tongue at the vowel's edge,
your departure is the unimagined, the one thing to avoid.
I have felt its arid shape in my sternum for so long.   I
have never looked at it, or let it laugh. I   have
never sat with it and accepted its echoes. I scan
the street: none of the   headlights   turning   inquiry
to the silk tarmac are yours. Car-surface   a liquid
knife: I've never stopped   asking, asking   for your presence
to continue. I am still here asking as time and excuses
lengthen themselves into the evening like
cats. I will always be here after everything ends.
Purple-tipped grasses   loop a   softness   through
these fields; my outsides catch   glare in the weirdest way.
I imagine a graphic of your car dispersing into wind, undoing
its sea-crumpled wings. How   does a person disappear?
The evening has an underneath. The evening   disappears
underneath people,   disappearance   is an   evening,
we disappear entire evenings because we are those
kinds of people; it's that simple. Evenings people
disappear. Evenings, people: disappear. No.

Rime / Ripe

At the top of the inhalation
there is swoop & confluence,
a peak forest-soft from above.

I fought with you
in my head & made it spindrift:
maybe somewhere

in the narrowing bend
of flu season there's a frozen river
underfoot. Maybe I am likeable

when a compound word:
today I found a late ambering
we couldn't classify,

downloaded that app
that's like Shazam for plants,
found the entry for

'orange banana tomato.' *Now,*
that is just three existing fruits,
I thought. *That is just inadmissible.*

New terms refused, we let skin
become patina-glittered in a future,
find itself an evergreen mouth.

Speak Up

Steeped in blue, I put a microphone to a breaking heart:
One day, I will bury my mother. Selfishly,

& with fear, I think:
She can bury me first.

I travel the length of this red trajectory, balance
on the arc of the story, asking,

Miracle baby at what cost?

I try to pull a single thread from the music:
the bright yellow pillow

cushioning the skull. Sunbeams *&* a face
like the middle of a flower.

I imagine it being lowered:
a ship on fire.

Children Should Be Seen & Never Heard

I was going to read to you
but decided words remained

more beautiful held in the jaw
of a page.

Narrow, cinnamon girl

finds being heard
more embarrassing
than her naked body.

They tell me,
When you are too open,
withdrawal moves

from escape to forgiveness.

At the Expense of Girls
for king puck

Like a toast,
irreversibly changed

by a sequence of teeth.
In a dream, they separate

wide enough for a coin.
He tells me, inside of him

are two anxious dogs.
Split a lip choking

out a howl. Face
caked in paint:

childlike, crayoned prince.
Moon out in the morning,

between your toes.

Murmuration

The chaos is green,

so green, you'd think it was the lodestar

with a neon sign for the end of the world, but NO WAY –

the blue just keeps blooming with birds. A method in this madness,

in this murmuration so bright, you'd think an enormous

old tree decided to lend the sky its leaves.

They tell you there is still time. Don't you dare think otherwise.

The future is a noisy and high-pitched place, thrilling with possibilities.

A great whoosh of them, shiny plumage, iridescent necks.

They insist there IS justice in the world, just listen,

because after the drought and the fire, come wet seasons.

Time is on the move and no matter what, there will always be tide.

The ebb and flow of budgerigars. How to explain this?

This explosion of sound and colour and sparks flying, spiralling, the vane turning

and turning, and good news travelling fast. For once, good news,

mesmerising news, flashing before you in the semaphore

of thousands of wings.

I have made a note of —

consciences being schlepped everywhere and that's life, blushing. You said: *Last time I saw you, your father was still alive, your good father.* My good father. As I walked up the hill I thought he'd be there to greet me but instead, there was this soft breeze, a blistering sky. My last poem was a kind of fury and I shredded every line. The poet goes on stage and announces *Time is skidding along, the word-shredding has begun.* We live in times of uncertainty. There was this grey hum in my thoughts, the opposite of laughter: it was the sound of listening to nothing at night. But we still write, we write, hold words to the light. You said: *I have to have something to live for! And a life to live!* Do you remember back when, two years ago? In my living room, next to the mirror, a neon green question mark flickers. Two years of locked hope and I-don't-know-what-to-say, and cycling past myself on a slow journey to nowhere. Day and night on the Peloton, the poet thinks of a landslide waiting to happen. Soon, there is a war. On the news, satellite images of *appalling acts,* sometimes *atrocities.* The poet makes a note of history and history and history repeating itself. The poet remembers her father who used to say *This war will end so badly. It will end so badly, this war, mark my words.* Before and after, we will be different people.

Hibiscus

Body my house / my horse my hound / what will I do / when you are fallen

— May Swenson

When I first touch my own body
it is want growing wild and soon my
fingers on slow-slow the wet soft house
petals and gasps and layers of electric oh my
where's my stallion oh god oh lovely horse
and sniffing at the lips of open bloom and my
pink sweet heat and now the hungry hound
of his bold mouth with the licking tongue and what
drips from it so loudly a trumpet so complete will
possess my voice which turns red purple and I
so smell the slippery blur of open close open do
more more with the crushed flower even when
I cry out even this bright colour of me on you
even when I and you are the sudden same are
blood drops soaking the final cry unpetalled fallen

Plainsong

Although reputedly illiterate, Cædmon, who tended livestock at Whitby monastery in the 7th century, is the earliest named English poet and is said to have received his calling in a dream

A rough wool blanket,
stockings of moss
my night vestments,

I sleep under beams
in this shed
on a bed of straw,

Cædmon the cowherd,
knowing only songs
from the hills:

moan of a mother
without her calf
in the early mist,

bullocks
munching grass
in the darkness.

I have no voice
in the supper hall,
no miracle tales,

no pretty poems
for the brothers' harp.
Pastures at birdcall

are heaven's music.
Christ in his kindness
lends me these words.

Time by Shadows

Nicolaus Kratzer, astronomer and clockmaker to Henry VIII

A finch on the grass
pecks a fallen apple,

ants in a hollow
strip a crippled bee,

a spider wraps a moth
too weak to leave the ground,

the orchard is fraying.
A sundial on the terrace

takes another heartbeat
from the afternoon

      shewing time by shadows,
      not only the hower of the day

      but months as they darken,
      a carved moone and starres.

Beneath a rowan tree,
watched by a nurse,

his child sleeps,
the seconds of her breath

too small to mark in stone.

On the Bridge

I.K. BRUNEL, ENGINEER, 1859
— Memorial inscription, Royal Albert Bridge, River Tamar

A hundred feet above the water
he counts the fortune
risked with every inch,

from bedrock
to painted trusses,
each stone of the towers.

Carried by couch
on a railway truck
he's surveying the site

one last time.
He has built the backbone
of a country

but can no longer walk.
The wagon stops
to let him see

the sweep of track,
an arch framing sky.
Below, the tide runs fast

against the piers;
up here, wind sharp
through the girders.

what happened | is happening again
in that this then there | of an event
recalled | so

carefully | the mind is obliged
to re- | cite the vision
witnessed | into rote

the tongue ties | that metal taste
to what | happened
sensing | my thoughts are

necessarily | bound
by the blood | in my mother's hair
that stiffens into | an accusation

I have long ignored | tainting
how | I see myself

I see myself | being seen
the impression | of a wound

the blood | in my mother's hair
that part of me | that I place

by memory | as one stroke
set against another | hardly

dry | drying hard
to fit | this form of words

grasping at | the subject
in hand | those brown curls

made black | wetly matted
crusting to a scab | that won't

heal | for days
livid | and still there

and still there | is this
lasting | that never before
and not after | of something
un- | understood

the idea | that I make
a problem of | the world
solving the un- | necessary
violence | by conceiving it

wrongly | what am I
trying to mean | this
for | I can't imagine
who could read this | just

as I want it read | as if
it happened | to someone else

PROSE

One

Imagine this:

Your body is a house stripped from the pages of a Gothic novel. There was a fire once, in the hearth of the home, and it burned through the soft furnishings. It took with it the comfort of crushed velvet curtains and the grand armchairs you once enjoyed quiet afternoons in. The books – oh, the books you lost: *Great Expectations*, *Persuasion*, *As I Lay Dying*. The shelves bowed against the heat and were buried under the weight of hot paperbacks and hard covers. Your body – the house, that is – became an origami structure where one room folded or fell neatly into another. Things that were once upstairs now sat in the belly of the building. The skylight was no longer a panel but the whole head of your structure; fragmented and gaping with crisp white remains around the edges. Cracks between blown-out windows and their frames whistled with every wind that ran through you, and for a long time that was the only noise.

The authorities investigated what had caused the fire, citing several points of origin. The kitchen seemed the most likely space – with the wide-open mouths of angry pots and the fury of the stove. There was always something to be cut and cooked and force-fed, and it wouldn't surprise you if the constant stream of steaming foods had led to this structural collapse – it was a theory you kept to yourself even though others mentioned it, too. Although, of course, there were those who accused *you* of being the cause – as though you'd do such a thing, and to your own ~~body~~ home.

Two

Getting dressed in the morning isn't as easy as it used to be. Partly because you can't stand to look at your body in the mirror and partly because you can't not look at your body in the mirror. You make your ribs into a tally chart of days since you've done things: enjoyed a snack; eaten with your family; liked yourself. You can't get dressed quickly enough in clothes that are too big for you, but in being too big they hide that you're ~~too small~~ not small enough. It used to be an idle pleasure, seeing yourself smaller in things that used to be just right. Goldilocks was the first to teach us that finding things that are just right for ourselves can often lead to some kind of catastrophe though. So with that in mind maybe it's no wonder that you're trying something too small. *You tried too big already.* You shake that thought away – the intrusive one that speaks in your hard voice but not with a soft tongue – all the while thinking how right it is. You finish preparing yourself for the day by painting on a face that feels clown-like but everyone loves that you're wearing more make-up now. They call it "experimenting with your style" but it feels more like hiding in plain sight.

When you leave the bathroom, fully clothed and desperate for a cup of tea, you collide with your mother in the hallway.

'Those clothes are getting too big for you,' she says.

'Oh, shush, they are not.'

'They are, love, I can see a real difference.'

This hurts you. You've never kept anything from her, not really. You may have hidden the occasional crafty smoke when you were younger, or the odd night out on the lash when you were "staying at a mate's and going straight to college". But everyone was hiding those sorts of things. The girls – when you were all young enough for it to be trendy – they tried to hide their eating disorders, too. In the same way that you grew out of your puppy fat, they grew out of their brittle bones and into their beautiful bodies. You did it the wrong way around, though, like a body-myth that shows the protagonist becoming thinner – weaker, more angular – as the story progresses. It feels like a regression when you think of it this way – as though a mental illness is something you're allowed when you're younger, but by the time you're pushing thirty you should know better.

'These clothes are as old as the hills, Mum, they're just stretched out.'

'Well, we should get you some new ones then.'

'But these are comfortable.' She'll have an answer for this – there's one for everything – so you try to cut the chord of one conversation in favour of another. 'Do you want a brew, anyway? I'm desperate for a drink.'

'Yeah, will you bring it up?'

'Course.'

You love the quiet of the morning downstairs. For a while you don't have to think about anything but the task at hand, which is usually answering emails, and taking phone calls. You're working remotely now – it's a brave new world, mid-pandemic – which means you don't have to contend with colleagues either. You handle several social media accounts for a small advertising company, although you're one of many helping hands at the job, so the company hasn't really felt small for a while. There's enough to keep you all busy and out of each other's ways, bar the occasional instant message to ask something that isn't usually related to work.

While the kettle boils you lean back against the kitchen counter. You pretend not to notice how uncomfortable the work surface is against the braille of your spine. The garden looks beautiful. You've put a lot of effort into scattering seeds liberally about the place and hoping for the best, and it seems to have really paid off. There are small wild gardens appearing in clusters, as though each set of seeds has formed a faction, and you wonder whether they're planning to overthrow the sunflowers.

There's so much food on the work surface. It's nothing offensive or drastic; nothing that you wouldn't eat – if you could stand to. There's a glass biscuit jar packed full of custard creams, hobnobs, rich tea, digestives. Smaller jars have smaller sweets; chocolate buttons, ice gems, raisins, peanuts. Your mum hasn't had a sit-down conversation with you about food, but oh, she's talking about it. You eye each container up and down like a suspect in a criminal case and you consider trying to convince yourself to eat something. But it's only mid-morning and you know you can do better than this.

When the kettle's boil whistles to a close you make the drinks and treat this as a distractor task. You're aware eating is important – you understand how the human body works, that is – but there are lots of other important things in the world that also aren't being done. On days like today that feels like a justification for leaving your stomach empty. Although you've arrived at a point in your "recovery" where you no longer know whether you want to feel empty, or full – nor do you know whether these words have anything to do with food.

You take hardly any milk in your tea; your mum takes a lot in hers. On your way back through the kitchen towards the stairs, you leave your own cuppa on the desk to wait, to cool. You can hear the chattering of a phone call overhead – your mum and one of the many insurance companies she's having to contend with mid-pandemic – and you hope this means she won't ask *the* question. And yet–

'Have you eaten something?' She covers the speaker to ask.

You bite back an eye roll. 'I'll have a cereal bar when I go downstairs.' You won't. You'll unwrap a cereal bar, cover it carefully in swathes of tissue and bury it at the bottom of the bin. Then you'll strategically leave the wrapper on the top of the rubbish pile, making sure that it's an unavoidable eye-catcher for whoever uses the bin next. This is how you don't eat breakfast now.

'Tea break later?'

'Sure, I've got an important call for work in around ten minutes, then a meeting.'

She understands your meaning. 'Yes, I'll be quiet.'

'Thanks, Mum.'

'Love you, kid.'

'You too.'

She's worried sick about you. There's a conversation to be had that neither of you are willing to initiate yet – it'll come, you're sure. But even without speaking you can see small changes in her look; the way her eyebrows pull together in a near-constant frown. When she hugs you now, you can't help but feel as though she's sizing you up. You've become Gretel, too skinny to do anything of use with and so everyone around you tries to feed you, without telling you the real reason for why. Sometimes you fantasise about them putting you in a mixing pot and boiling you down to nothing. It's when you think about things like that you realise food isn't about food at all; it's about magic. You'd like to make yourself the disappearing woman/man. Like those famous illusionists who make their bodies origami, corners and edges tight enough to stash into a box. But when your curtain is lifted you'd like to not be there at all.

Your tea is cool enough to drink by the time you're at your desk. You've got a good six minutes before the phone starts ringing so you take in greedy mouthfuls (oh, greed, now you're The Ungrateful Son, and you wonder whether the Grimms might put a forever-frog on your face to stop you from ~~not~~ eating). The fairytale references are many in your head. You spent a significant portion of your life studying them – a waste of a degree if ever there was one, your sibling ~~says~~ jokes – but they help you to see things differently. Your counsellor calls it transference. You call it getting through the day.

By the time the phone rings you're two thirds of the way through your cup of tea and you're glad because you always forget to drink during these conversations – sometimes breathe, too, but that's down to the crying. Your counsellor says it will get easier. But they're bound to say that, aren't they?

Belly of Irreversibles

I was never allowed to tell people where I lived. This was because I lived in a bad area. Other things were classified as bad, but they were always plural. There was only one bad area: the one I lived in.

I now live in a good area. I am still working-class.

Sitting in a hotel breakfast room on Renfrew Street in Glasgow, I heard a loud ring tone rattling out from the kitchen, it was *The Sash*. I told the person I was with what I was hearing but they didn't understand so I had to explain what *The Sash* is and how it sickens and scares working-class Northern Irish Catholics of my generation. I was careful to keep my voice down, so the person in the kitchen with *The Sash* ringtone wouldn't hear me, wouldn't poison my breakfast, wouldn't try to kill me. I had completely lost my appetite. When the full Scottish fried breakfast (I had ordered before hearing *The Sash* ringtone) arrived I gulped down every scrap, so nothing went to waste. I was tempted to drink the milk in the little jug too, because it was free and that was what I used to be told to do when I was growing up, for the calcium. I did not do this because I was worried the person I was with (someone who I already knew well at that time, who is still infact a friend and who is also working-class) would judge me. I was calibrating what magnitude of working-class behaviour was acceptable and how working-class my friend was, compared to how working-class I was. I didn't want to disgrace myself.

When I went to primary school I could already read and count. My wonderful father had taught me; he was always unemployed (as were the majority the other men in the bad area) so he was about alot. The primary school class of thirty-three was divided into different reading groups, apparently according to aptitude. I was put into the lowest ability group because of the bad area I lived in. I knew this was unfair, for me and for the others, but I could not prove they could read, I could only prove I could read.

The first thing I want to know about people is what class they are. I don't believe in social mobility: you are always the same class as the one you grew up in even if your circumstances have radically changed. It is relatively easy in the UK to work out what class people are, if you've got the appetite for it. However, when you start working abroad (which if you've actioned your spiralling upwardly mobile aspirations well enough, then you will be) it is almost impossible that you are grasping the nuance of detectable signifiers of another country's class system. You simply cannot be as sure as you would like to be. This is actually a pretty constricting way to be in the world.

On the rare occasions I was offered a lift home from school by the mother of one of my middle-class schoolmates, I always had to tell them I lived in a different area, an area three tiers better than my own, but a working-class area nonetheless so I would appear credible. These mothers with cars, for it was never the fathers, would bring me to where I asked them to and then drop me off. I would wait until they had driven quite a way off, assuring them I was fine, and then I walked the long walk home. It would have been much quicker just to have walked straight back from school. I knew they knew I was lying because each mother only ever offered once and then never again. This made me feel ashamed. Ashamed I had to lie, but not ashamed about the bad area I lived in, because I knew this was not my fault.

One of my middle-class friends asked me to her house for dinner after one time. She lived quite far away from where the primary school was, but it was ok because there was a school bus that took the middle-class children to their area, there was of course no bus taking the working-class children to our area. I was very excited and, surely it goes without saying, also very nervous. Her whole family was sitting around a giant kitchen table in a kitchen, the table was basically the footprint of the lower floor of my whole house. Her mother served the father first, a great big slab of juicy looking steak, a mound of boiled potatoes with the skins on, and a pile of buttery cabbage. I'd never had steak before in real life, it looked really delicious. But, I was not served steak, I was served sausages. To be fair, everyone except the father was served sausages so I was not being deliberately left out. However, I was still extremely disappointed and could not understand why different members of the family got different food, and why the father had been served first. In my house, children were always fed first, were given the best bits of the cheap food we had, the parents took the scraps. The implication being: our children will die if they are not fed. Families in the bad area I grew up in fed all children this way, not just their own.

I note how often other writers evoke a relatively well-known Greek myth to lend gravity and longitudinal context to their subject. You'll start noticing it too, now that I've drawn your attention to it, you probably have already anyway, maybe you even like it, sometimes I like it myself actually. I try to summon a Greek myth to dance teasingly in this text (like the woman from the opening credits of *Tales of the Unexpected*) to give my subject the dignity I think it deserves. Sisyphus immediately comes to mind, because… well you know… it's obvious. Prometheus, I have a fancy for the raging symbolism of fire and the image of his luscious regenerating liver. Antigone's moral grandeur seduces then mocks me with its completeness.

The working-class way is fragmentary and composed of glittery remnants: Harp lager can ring pulls, shattered glass, pearlescent phlegm streaked with blood.

The rest of that day in Glasgow I kept thinking about the leftover milk in the little jug in the hotel breakfast room, of it being poured down the sink: the awful waste.

I had an argument with a friend once about innate cultural value. I gave the example of how *Metal Mickey* is as important as *Jules et Jim* because, I said, it has to do with the analytical eye you are casting over the content, not the content itself. I knew my example was facetious and a wee bit silly but I really felt it. I still really feel it. I chose *Jules et Jim* rather than another more obscure and probably interesting film to me (even when I was child) like say *Come and See* or *Themroc* or *Shellshock Rock* because I thought they would have been more likely to have seen *Jules et Jim*, so yes, I was sort of patronising them. They snorted, I mean they literally snorted with derision.

Taste is actually quite easy to learn.

It was only when I started mixing with middle-class people I realised drinking excessive amounts of alcohol can bloat you. The neighbours I had grown up beside in the bad area (mainly men, the ones who drank excessive amounts of alcohol, most did not) were emptied out by it. There was nothing left of them. I never questioned where they got the money to buy the drink, I didn't know how much drink cost anyway.

A friend told me about someone they know who used to get a raw jelly cube in their school lunchbox as a sweet treat. They told me this because they were trying to explain how poor the other person was. They were trying to be nice. They also told me because, well let's face it, it is a funny image: bouncy. I laughed to be polite and because, as I've just said there, it is quite amusing. But what I was really thinking was: I would rather have had a raw jelly cube than a free school dinner.

I probably don't need to tell you here about the necessity and the indignity of free school dinners. All you need to know, incase you don't already, is that the tickets for free school dinners were a different colour than the tickets for ordinary school dinners.

I am disgusted and overwhelmed by the idea of wastefulness, yet I think I waste a lot of my time. I think this is because my time feels like it costs nothing. I am my own resource. I use myself. I wear myself out. I'm doing it now, for you, on this page.

I. I. I. I. I was introducing the guest film I had selected to be shown at a festival when, standing at the mic just about to speak, it occurred to me, that what I am really interested in is working-classness as method.

If you've grown up very poor working-class, it's relatively straightforward to describe the slight portions of poverty (the half full milk jug, the jelly cube, and yes, they are often calibrated by food, I mean, honest to god, how could they not be) but it's so very hard to explain the essential distinctiveness of working-classness and how it burrows under your nails. I bite my nails so I am speaking figuratively but it does feel like a burrowing, like a *ceremony*.

Into the mic I said: What I am really interested in is working-classness as method. I was surprised it came out. Afterwards, quite a lot of people came up to me, asking, in a genuine way, what I meant by working-classness as method. All I wondered was: Why are they so fucking interested?

Tantalus, I should have summoned Tantalus!

And I return to this question regularly. What does working-classness as method actually mean? And who cares about it, apart from people like me. And again, I'm here with it now, in this text, clattering the tin bones of being working-class. How you go about things; how you imagine something will turn out; the expectant emotion of change; wanting but never being sure.

I told my mother about *The Sash* ringtone incident in Glasgow. I told her because I had little else to talk with her about and was trying to fill time on the telephone. Her voice was stiff: a fatal mix of indignation and incomprehension. Did you give them your real name? Yes, of course I'd given them my real name, I had to, I'd been invited to give a public lecture. Why? But why did you give them your real name? She was trying to be helpful. But what else could I have done, hadn't I been invited to be *myself*.

Will Power

Remember me, hanging from the rock?

It's the end of summer and my resources are low. I jumped into the season headfirst this year, desperate to do things I've never thought necessary, never felt the rush to do. The sea has always been there, the mountains aren't moving, the veins of electricity beneath and above us continue to hum, the wind is always waiting to tear through your coat and whisk you away.

This summer, I really needed to feel it. To be in it. To push my hands into the soil, lie flat on the grass, and let the Earth's energy swell up into my muscles, to let the wind steal my breath and return it tenfold, and to feel the sea tug at my fears and roll me back to the shoreline. To look Wylfa in the eye and not back down.

When they asked me to step forward and get fitted for the harness, I could barely stand. My condition, whatever it is, had flared up, aggravated by me ignoring it, pushing myself to go out and explore the island, the mainland, the power in the land. I had already shovelled as many painkillers into my mouth as I could safely take. Had sat down at every opportunity, feeling like my limbs were made of stone. I looked up at the rock face, at the children whizz up and down its stony features, and it seemed ten times higher than I knew it was. I'd already given up my place in the queue once, gifting a little girl the chance to test her developing limbs on another plane.

But there was the man holding out the helmet, shaking the harness, smiling at me. He could see, behind the mask of pain and the frown of exhaustion, that there was a little girl in me shouting *Come on! When are you going to get the chance to engage so completely with these mountains again? Next year you'll be older, even more tired. This could be it! Get off your backside and get up there!*

So I got up.

The crack of my knees was like wood spitting in fire as I straightened and stepped forward. My legs slid into the thick straps of the harness and the helmet tightened around my head.

I met my son's steady stare, his triumph of conquering the wall still glowing in his cheeks, his expectation of my achievement burning in his eyes.

I looked at the person belaying, tried to calculate our contrasting body mass. If I let go, slip or lose my grip, would I plummet while he rose? Would I smash to the earth like a conker? Lose my mobility in one fell swoop instead of through years of degeneration?

He reassured me, pointed to the first foothold, smiled. Couldn't see the effort it took to step forward, can't understand how much harder this climb would be for me than for the fizzing balls of energy that chatter to their parents behind me.

Are you okay? he asked.

I'm fine.

Kept my smile fixed, kept the pain invisible. Gripped the first crevice with fear-slicked fingers and hauled myself up. Each stretch and grasp drawing glucose from my blood, adrenalin surging, masking pain.

I looked up, saw the knotted rope I have to reach, the bell a burnished curve in dying light. I could feel the eyes of my son and husband like an energy boost.

I kept going, my heart thumping like a wind turbine, the sway of my body rocking gently like the tide. Harnessed every memory that the earth had given me over the last few months as I sucked air into exhausted lungs, the oxygen feeding my tissues. The sun on my freckled arms, determination smouldering in my core…

I am close, but not close enough. I stop and look at the line of rope rising six more feet above me.

I'm done.

Here I am, clinging on.

I'm lichen, I'm moss, I'm the trembling tree rooted in the memory of soil beside me.

And I'm tired.

I want to give up, to be slowly lowered back to solid ground and the supportive arm of my husband, to go home, to lie on the sofa, to rest.

I look down and see my son's face, small and round, pale as a jackdaw's eye against the black slate path. His voice is distant, dizzying. He knows I can do it because I can do anything. That's what parents do. He claps, and it sounds like thunder.

I turn back and hug the stone, ignore the man belaying for me who asks if I want to come down. I force another stretch from an aching arm. There is no adrenaline left.

I'm using borrowed energy. I'm sucking power from the rock itself. I'm not going down until I've touched the knotted rope at the top, rung that bell. I ignore the lactic acid in my thighs and push on. I feel the sun burning the back of my neck and reach higher. My teeth are aching from the pressure my jaws exert.

One last stretch.

The rope knot is rough in my sweat-slicked fingers. I cling to it and turn, wave a shaking arm at my miniature family. Let out a breath that shudders in my chest as it is released.

The bell chimes, a public accomplishment.

No one sees me kiss the rock or whisper a prayer of thanks into the breeze. I am filled with gratitude for the world around me, for the trees and soil and stone and sun and water and wind that led me here.

I know I'll never do this again; the only thing I'll take away is the increased throb of pain in my joints and a need to sleep longer than usual tonight.

And the memory. The knowledge that today, at least, my willpower was enough.

I descend. It takes only a few moments and my ears pop about halfway down. Little arms encircle my waist, and a big hand takes my own, steadies my steps over the loose rocks at the bottom. I step out of the harness and hand back the helmet. Summer is over.

I did it.

And that's enough for now.

6 years later, we're still laying out our unrest

Milton Keynes UK
Ingram Content Group UK Ltd.
UKHW011844010324
438745UK00008B/227